Encouraging Metacognition

Critical Pedagogical Perspectives

Greg S. Goodman, *General Editor*

Vol. 12

The Educational Psychology series is part of the Peter Lang Education list.
Every volume is peer reviewed and meets
the highest quality standards for content and production.

PETER LANG
New York • Washington, D.C./Baltimore • Bern
Frankfurt • Berlin • Brussels • Vienna • Oxford

Patricia Liotta Kolencik
& Shelia A. Hillwig

Encouraging Metacognition

SUPPORTING LEARNERS THROUGH METACOGNITIVE TEACHING STRATEGIES

PETER LANG
New York • Washington, D.C./Baltimore • Bern
Frankfurt • Berlin • Brussels • Vienna • Oxford

Library of Congress Cataloging-in-Publication Data
Kolencik, Patricia Liotta.
Encouraging metacognition: supporting learners through metacognitive
teaching strategies / Patricia Liotta Kolencik, Shelia A. Hillwig.
p. cm. — (Educational psychology: critical pedagogical perspectives; v. 12)
Includes bibliographical references and index.
1. Thought and thinking—Study and teaching. 2. Learning, Psychology of.
3. Metacognition. I. Hillwig, Shelia A. II. Title.
LB1590.3.K655   370.15'2—dc23   2011026113
ISBN 978-1-4331-1274-4 (hardcover)
ISBN 978-1-4331-1273-7 (paperback)
ISSN 1943-8109

Bibliographic information published by **Die Deutsche Nationalbibliothek**
Die Deutsche Nationalbibliothek lists this publication in the "Deutsche
Nationalbibliografie"; detailed bibliographic data is available
on the Internet at http://dnb.d-nb.de/.

Contents

INTRODUCTION

About This Book

Encouraging Metacognition: Supporting Learners through Metacognitive Teaching Strategies provides educators with practical teaching strategies for improving students' metacognitive knowledge and skills to enhance student learning. Our standards-based environment, as well as the current research in educational reform, supports the need for students to be able to use metacognition to ensure that they become autonomous, self-monitoring, independent, 21st century learners. It is the authors' hope that this text will empower educators with strategies to develop and extend students' metacognitive knowledge and skills to create these independent learners.

Drawn from a combination of the current research and our extensive educational backgrounds, the authors believe that the teaching and learning process not only involves cognitive operations, but also the dispositions to engage in these operations. We believe that all educators need to introduce strategies that promote metacognition. The intent of education is to foster students' desire and ability to be lifelong learners. The metacognitive strategies presented here provide teachers with repertoire necessary to add purpose and relevance to the learning process and give students the opportunity to contribute to thinking about their own learning.

A Word about the Book's Purpose

The essential questions upon which this book is written are:

"How can a teacher help students to become more effective, life-long, independent learners?" and "What does it take to reflect on what is necessary to learn?" The following quote from Stenmark (1989) provides the underlying purpose for writing this book and reflects these essential questions. "The capability and willingness to assess their own progress and learning is one of the greatest gifts students can develop. Those who are able to review their own performance, explain the reasons for choosing the processes they used, and identify the next step have a life-long head start." The authors believe that teachers can purposefully guide students' development of metacognitive skills by using the strategies suggested in this book. We believe that the teaching of metacognitive skills is essential for the 21st century.

Metacognition involves the monitoring and control of attitudes, such as students' beliefs about themselves, the value of persistence, the nature of work, and their personal responsibility in accomplishing a goal" (Fusco & Fountain, 1992, p.240). All of these characteristics are essential components to prepare students for real-life situations. The authors believe that metacognition, purposefully thinking about one's own thinking strategies, is an essential part of the learning triangle (curriculum, instruction, and assessment), and consequential for learners of all ages in order to empower them to "learn to think," and to "think to learn," thus, promoting the success of every student. Current research findings indicate that teaching metacognitive strategies to students can lead to a marked improvement in their achievement.

Teachers are accountable to equip students for the dynamic and uncertain circumstances that characterize life in the 21st century competitive global workplace. Those who will succeed in the 21st century global community are those who learn to think. Today's students need to acquire skills that will help them successfully navigate the complex and constantly changing territory of the future. They need skills that will not become obsolete. They need to have mental processes and structures in their toolbox to survive and thrive. We believe that the teaching of metacognitive skills falls into the 21st century toolbox and teachers have an obligation to amplify and enhance their ability to teach these essential skills in order to make learning more meaningful and relevant for our students.

A Word about the Book's Organization

The book is divided into three parts. The first part presents an overview of the concept of metacognition by describing its dimensions, distinctiveness, and importance as supported by the literature.

The first chapter, Metacognition: A Bit of Theory includes an explanation of what metacognition is and is not; the components of metacognition; and why it is vital to the learning process.

The second chapter, The Language of Thinking and Thinking Strategies, examines the language that implements the teaching of thinking. It discusses verbal, written, and graphic languages that assist in thinking across disciplines to build students' thought processes in order to conduct themselves most effectively as learners. Moreover, this chapter presents the language of thinking to inspire independent learning to create and foster the culture and community of a thoughtful classroom.

The second part offers five metacognitive teaching strategies for use in the classroom that promote metacognition: thinking aloud, thinking journals, thinking words (mnemonics), thinking maps, and thinking with reading. This section describes each strategy and details how to incorporate and implement the strategy in one's daily practice. Each strategy concentrates on fundamental and transparent ways to enable one to use the strategy by providing the mechanisms for the teacher to act as a role model and contribute to the improvement of learning.

Chapter 3, Thinking Aloud, concentrates on the "think aloud" approach, one of the most common strategies associated with metacognition. This strategy calls for a cognitive monologue on behalf of the teacher and requires students to verbalize their thoughts.

Chapter 4, Thinking Journals, tackles the use of journals for assessing the reflectiveness of students' responses, evidence of transfer to other classes or life outside of school, and students' ability to plan, monitor, and self-evaluate.

Chapter 5, Thinking with Mnemonics, looks at using mnemonic tools such as rhymes, acrostics, acronyms, and charting, not only to help students remember content, but also to construct, connect and relate their thinking to content.

Chapter 6, Thinking Maps, investigates thinking maps, also known as graphic organizers or concept maps, presented as an effective metacognitive strategy used to visually organize ideas and illustrate relationships to launch and guide classroom discussion and as a visual representation of the thought processes used when studying content.

Chapter 7, Thinking as a Reader, examines explicit instructional strategies in order for students to become metacognitive readers who can effectively make necessary text to text, text to self, and text to world connections.

Each chapter in Part Two begins with the essential questions, "What Are The Nuts and Bolts?" and "What Does The Research Say?" These opening sections define the strategy in detail and provide the evidence of effectiveness for each strategy.

Unique to the book's chapters in this part is the use of the prefix "META" as a common framework to learn about each strategy's context. Webster's dictionary states that the prefix "meta" represents after, beyond, or higher. The authors contend that the strategies presented in this book challenge the reader to do just that. Teachers will reflect after teaching and students' thinking will be improved after integrating the strategies. Students are being stretched beyond their current frame of thinking and moving toward the completion of much higher level tasks. The prefix sums up the heartbeat of the book. The framework's legend is as follows:

- "M" represents the word "model."
  The "M" segment details methods for "modeling" the strategy in the classroom, i.e., demonstrating appropriate behaviors or skills that the teacher wants their students to learn.
- "E" represents the word "engage."
  The "E" segment details strategies for promoting student engagement, supporting students' construction of their own learning, and motivating them to become active learners.
- "T" represents the word "transfer."
  The "T" segment details methods to take the acquired knowledge, skill, or understanding in one situation and apply it to a new or different situation. Transfer is critical to success in school life and life well beyond the walls of the schoolhouse.
- "A" represents the word "assess."
  The "A" segment details strategies to determine and evaluate learner outcomes. Learner can be used here to identify the teacher as learner or the student as the learner. When appropriate, reflections for the teacher are included in order for the teacher-learner to assess his or her own success with implementation of the strategy in the classroom.

The authors hope that this framework will assist the reader in understanding how to incorporate and implement the strategy in one's daily practice. Because the framework addresses the essential instructional aspects of model, engage and assess, the strategies presented are comprehensive and straightforward.

Each chapter in Part Two concludes with a section entitled "Classroom Snapshot: On Your Own." The purpose of this snapshot section, consisting of four inquiry-based questions, is to provide an opportunity for the reader to reflect on the chapter's content. This reflection supports self-assessment and promotes transfer into daily teaching, which requires the teachers' own metacognition.

The final section, "Investigating Further," contains an annotated bibliography of print and web resources to find additional information on the strategy.

The third part entitled "Metacognition in Action" contains three chapters. Chapter 8, "Meta-Q: Thinking About Questioning, discusses the art of questioning as an effective practice worthy of development in the quest for enhanced metacognition. This chapter considers both teacher-generated and student-generated questioning since both aspects play an important role in strengthening metacognition and moves the learner toward higher-level, complex thinking resulting in self-refection, self-monitoring, and self-regulating.

Chapter 9 , Meta-S: Thinking While Studying," focuses on a repertoire of study skills strategies, habits, and attitudes to assist students' success in "learning how to learn" in a variety of situations both in school and in life. The chapter stresses study strategies to help students achieve that success and develop a feeling of accomplishment and self-worth.

Chapter 10, Thinking Actively: More Metacognitive Strategies, contains a plethora of active learning strategies designed to help teachers develop, encourage, and facilitate students' metacognitive skills. The strategies are practical and generic in nature, thus, can be adapted to teach any subject across the curriculum. These strategies enable deeper learning, understanding, and reflection of content and concepts on the part of the student. The strategies discussed in this section ask students to demonstrate their understanding by applying multiple academic skills such as interpreting visual information, conducting an analysis, using criteria, making inferences, and writing coherent explanations.

Additionally, appendices and index are included. Appendix A, "Thinking as a Learner: Best Practices," contains best practices teachers can incorporate into their daily routine to promote and encourage the development of metacognitive skills. Appendix B, "Thinking as a Learner: Self-monitoring Checkbric", is a self-monitoring tool that contains questions to help students develop metacognitively and reflect on their learning. Appendix C: "Thinking as a Learner: Metacognitive Rubric," presents a sample rubric on metacognition that can be used in the classroom to lead students toward initiation of a metacognitive monologue of study skills in order to become life-long, independent learners and strategic thinkers.

A Word about the Intended Audience

This researched-based resource is designed for a variety of educators: the K-12 classroom teacher; curriculum specialists; academic coaches, reading specialists, school librarians, administrators, teacher educators, and teacher-candidates. It will equip educators with insightful metacognitive strategies to challenge students to "learn to think" and to "think to learn." This book will help teachers develop learners to survive and thrive in today's complex global environment.

A Final Thought

Encouraging Metacognition: Supporting Learners through Metacognitive Teaching Strategies offers a variety of researched-based strategies that will motivate your students to become actively engaged in the thinking and learning process Although metacognitive strategies may already be in your repertoires, the strategies presented in this text illustrate how these strategies fit seamlessly into your curriculum regardless of your content area; thus, producing a metacurriculum.

The authors believe that one of keys to education is helping students not only to learn content, but also to learn a rich repertoire of strategies to become creative, reflective thinkers. Teaching students to think about thinking is the ultimate goal. The objective of education is thinking, and learning is a consequence of thinking.

REFERENCES

Fusco, E., & Fountain, G. (1992). Reflective teacher, reflective learner. In A. Costa, J. Bellanca, & R. Fogarty (Eds.) *If minds matter: A foreword to the future* (Vol. 1, pp. 238-255). Palatine, Ill.: Skylight.

Stenmark, J. K. (1989). *Assessment alternatives in mathematics: An overview of assessment techniques that promote learning.* Berkeley, CA: EQUALS.

SECTION ONE

Background Information

CHAPTER ONE

Metacognition: A Bit of Theory

Kolencik/Hillwig

Many people are unaware of their own thinking process. "Some people are unaware of their own thinking processes while they are thinking. When asked, "How are you solving that problem? They may reply, 'I don't know, I'm just doing it... .' they can't describe the steps and sequences that they use before, during or after problem solving."

Costa, 1991, p. 23

This section presents an overview of the concept of metacognition by describing its dimensions, distinctiveness, and importance. The authors believe that understanding the underpinnings of metacognition to the point of being able to effectively teach metacognitive strategies is an integral part of the teaching and learning process. Thus, we have presented a bit of the theoretical background.

What is it?

- Thinking about thinking
- Learning how to learn
- Knowing how to learn
- Controlling one's own learning
- Regulating one's own learning though planning, monitoring, evaluating and reflecting on one's learning
- Self-awareness of knowledge construction
- "Knowing what to do, when to do it, how to do it, and what to take into consideration" (DeBono, 1976, p. 51)

Metacognition... If one were asked to provide a definition for the term metacognition, the standard definition is "thinking about one's thinking." Although this simple response is quite acceptable, the authors have chosen to provide more precise definitions from scholars, researchers, and cognitive psychologists to clarify, enhance, and expand the concept of metacognition to provide the reader with additional insight into this complex concept.

The word metacognition is composed of two words: "meta" and "cognition." The prefix *meta* comes from the Greek and means "about." The term "metacognition" can be traced in the literature to the late seventies where Flavell (1976) first used the word "metacognition". He describes it in these words:

> "Metacognition refers to one's knowledge concerning one's own cognitive processes or anything related to them, e.g., the learning-relevant properties of information or data. For example, I am engaging in metacognition if I notice that I am having more trouble learning A than B; if it strikes me that I should double check C before accepting it as fact" (Flavell, 1976, p. 232).

Since that time scholars, researchers, and cognitive psychologists have proposed more precise definitions of metacognition. Reading through these definitions, you will find that the simple definition of metacognition, "thinking about one's thinking," becomes more elaborate.

As you will see, the more specific descriptions from the literature include references to knowledge and control of factors that affect learning, such as knowledge of self, the task at hand, strategies to be employed (Baker & Brown, 1984; Palincsar & Brown, 1981) and planning, monitoring, and evaluating thinking processes (Dirkes, 1985). Swartz and Perkins (1989) define metacognition as "becoming aware of your thought processes in order to then control them when appropriate" (p. 11).

Fusco and Fountain (1992) further explain that metacognition involves the monitoring and control of attitudes, such as students' beliefs about themselves, the value of persistence, the nature of work, and their personal responsibility in accomplishing a goal" (p. 240). These aspects fall under the umbrella of dispositions for thinking and learning and these characteristics are essential components to prepare students for real-life situations.

What Is It Not?

Metacognition should not be confused with critical thinking; however, critical thinkers will most likely employ some metacognitive strategies, even if it is unknowingly. Metacognitive strategies can be employed with higher level and critical thinking, as well as with the lower cognitive levels. Metacognitive strategies can be used with the two lowest levels of Bloom's Taxonomy, knowledge and comprehension. The difference is being cognizant of one's own thinking.

As educators, we cannot assume that our learners are using metacognition, simply because they appear to be implementing higher-level thinking. Being able to recognize and discuss their thinking may be one of the most difficult tasks that they will have encountered. "Metacognitive skills include taking conscious control of learning, planning and selecting strategies, monitoring the progress of learning, correcting errors, analyzing the effectiveness of learning strategies, and changing learning behaviors and strategies when necessary." (Ridley et al., 1992, p. 293).

Components of Metacognition

According to Baker and Brown (1984) metacognition appears to involve two basic components: 1) students' awareness of the processes they need to successfully complete a task, and 2) students' cognitive monitoring—the ability to determine if the task is being completed correctly and make corrections as appropriate.

In his work, *Dimensions of Thinking*, Marzano (1988) discusses these two essential components of metacognition: 1) knowledge and control of self, and 2) knowledge and control of process. Winn and Snyder (1996) elaborate on these components by indicating that two basic processes occur simultaneously: *monitoring your progress* as you learn, and *making changes and adapting* your strategies if you perceive you are not doing so well. According to them, metacognition is about self-reflection, self-responsibility, and self-awareness, as well as goal setting and time management.

In sum, metacognition, the awareness of the *process of learning*, is a critical ingredient to successful teaching and learning. Metacognition is a key variable that differentiates effective thinkers from less effective thinkers and involves choosing the best way to approach a learning task, i.e., self-monitoring. Metacognition includes the ability to know when and why to apply different strategies to study or solve different problem types. Students with effective metacognitive skills set goals, organize their activities, select among various approaches to learning, and change strategies when needed. Metacognition is *purposefully* thinking about one's own thinking strategies and knowing how to learn.

Developmental Differences in Metacognition

According to Alexander, Carr, and Schwanenflugel, (1995), metacognition is a difficult cognitive skill and requires time to develop; thus, teachers need to be aware of some developmental differences in order to use metacognitive strategies effectively.

Research findings show significant developmental differences in the growth, proficiency and refinement of metacognitive skills. Young children, by age 5 or 6, know that familiar items are easier to understand than unfamiliar ones, that short lists are easier to remember than long ones, that recognition is easier than recall, and that forgetting is more likely to occur as time goes by (Lyon & Flavell, 1993). As children mature, they are more likely to determine if they have understood instruction (Markman, 1979) or if they have studied enough to remember a set of items (Flavell et al., 1970). Older students are more aware of the relationships between attention and learning and of the need to focus on relevant materials; they are also better at ignoring distracting stimuli than younger students (Mokhtari & Reichard, 2002).

To this end, there is great variability in metacognitive skills, even among students of the same age. Perkins (1992) defined four levels of metacognitive learners: tacit, aware, strategic, and reflective. Tacit learners are unaware of their metacognitive knowledge. Aware learners know about some of the kinds of thinking they do—generating ideas, finding evidence—but not strategic in their thinking. Strategic learners organize their thinking by using problem solving, decision making, evidence seeking, and other types of strategies. Reflective learners not only are strategic about their thinking, but also reflect on their thinking in progress, ponder their strategies and revise them. In sum, teachers need to be aware of students' developmental differences and levels in the teaching of metacognitive skills.

Studies show that increases in learning have followed direct instruction in metacognitive strategies. These results suggest that direct teaching of these thinking strategies may be useful, and that independent use develops gradually (Scruggs, 1985). Likewise, according to Schunk (2008) having effective metacognitive skills can compensate for lower ability, thus, teaching metacognitive skills can be especially helpful to students who are underperformers in school because metacognitive ability does not seem to be related to other intellectual abilities.

Why Should We Teach Metacognitive Skills and Why Are Metacognitive Strategies So Important?

The literature is replete with findings about the impact that teaching metacognitive skills has on improving student achievement. The following research findings support the importance of teaching metacognitive skills and provide a rock solid answer to the question why we should teach such skills.

- Students' control of cognition can significantly improve their cognitive processing and learning (Azevedo, Greene, & Moos, 2007).
- Teaching metacognitive strategies to students can lead to a marked improvement in their achievement (Alexander, Graham, & Harris, 1998; Hattie et al., 1996).

The importance of developing metacognitive learners has also been noted in the work of Tomlinson and McTighe (2006). They state "the most effective learners are metacognitive" (p. 79). In other words, these learners are cognizant of their own learning. They are aware of their learning styles; they monitor their own performance; and they establish their learning goals. Strategic learners are able to manage their time wisely and demonstrate organizational skills as well. Effective learners don't just stumble onto success, but strategically pursue it and change strategies when needed. Learners that are less effective have difficulty identifying their learning preferences and the strategies that they employ.

The whole purpose of teaching metacognitive strategies is to increase students' self-awareness about what it takes to learn. Metacognitive processes include knowledge about oneself as a learner, knowledge about academic tasks, and knowledge about strategies to use in order to accomplish those academic tasks.

As students become more skilled at using metacognitive strategies, they gain confidence and become more independent as learners. Independence leads to ownership as students realize they can pursue their own intellectual needs and discover a world of information at their fingertips. The task of educators is to acknowledge, cultivate, and enhance the metacognitive capabilities of all learners.

Where to Begin

The good news is that metacognitive strategies can be taught and developed in all learners and the benefits of this effort can be clearly noted as the aforementioned research supports.

Costa (1991), an expert in improving education through more thoughtful instruction and assessment, indicates that teachers must teach for, of, and about thinking in their classrooms. Costa asserts that prior to teaching for thinking you must set the stage, i.e., develop and establish a classroom climate that is conducive to teaching for thinking i.e., the thoughtful classroom. Costa suggests the following as effective starting points:

- Posing problems, raising questions, creating dilemmas, and inviting students to engage in problem solving
- Positively responding to students' ideas, listening carefully to their thoughts, and helping them to clarify and understand their thinking
- Remaining nonjudgmental while students explore ideas
- Encouraging experimentation and risk taking
- Modeling good thinking strategies in your teaching
- Interacting with students, colleagues, and parents.
- Helping students understand why they solve problems correctly or why their ideas about how to do something do not work
- Helping students to understand which learning strategies work best for them: auditory, visual, or kinesthetic.

A Final Word

As we have seen, metacognition, the awareness of the process of learning, is a critical ingredient to successful teaching and learning. Metacognition is a key variable that differentiates effective thinkers from less effective thinkers and involves choosing the best way to approach a learning task. Students with effective metacognitive skills set goals, organize their activities, select among various approaches to learning, and change strategies if needed. It is as important for educators to help students identify effective strategies as to help those who are struggling academically. It is in these situations that teacher modeling and explicit instruction in metacognition come into play.

Best practice literature tells us that powerful learning comes from cognitive experiences. We know that many teachers have moved well beyond the "chalk and talk, drill and kill" approach believing that recall and memorization do not constitute real understanding. Instead, today's effective teachers are developing lessons that emphasize specific types of thinking to improve student learning; such as drawing inferences, synthesis, hypothesizing, analytical reasoning, inquiry, interpretation, metaphorical thinking, and creative design, to name a few. Along with these skills, is metacognition, the view that students can become increasingly aware of their own thinking. Thus, teachers must help students and provide opportunities for them to become conscious of their own cognitive process and assist them in better monitoring their work as well as their thinking. The bottom line is that students need to develop the ability to self-monitor and become independent learners.

REFERENCES

Alexander, G. A., Graham, S., & Harris, K. R. (1998). A perspective on strategy research: Progress and prospects. *Educational Psychology Review*, 10(2), 129-154.

Alexander, J. M., Carr, M., & Schwanenflugel, P. J. (1995). Development of metacognition in gifted children: Directions for future research. *Developmental Review*, 15(1), 1-37.

Azevedo, R., Greene, J. A., & Moos, D. C. (2007). The effect of a human agent's external regulation upon college students' hypermedia learning. *Metacognition & Learning*, 2, 67-87.

Baker, L., & Brown, A. (1984). Metacognitive skills and reading. In P.D. Pearson (Ed.), *The Handbook of Reading Research* (pp. 353–94). New York: Longman.

Costa, A. L. (1991). *The school as a home for the mind: A collection of articles.* Palatine, IL: IRI/21Skyline Publishing.

DeBono, E. (1976). *Teaching Thinking.* London, England: Penguin, p. 51.

Dirkes, M. Ann. (1985, November). "Metacognition: Students in charge of their thinking." *Roeper Review*, 8(2), 96-100.

Flavell, J. H. (1976). Metacognitive aspects of problem solving. In L. B. Resnick (Ed.), *The nature of intelligence* (pp. 231-236). Hillsdale, NJ: Erlbaum.

Flavell, J. H., Friedrichs, A. G., & Hoyt, J. D. (1970). "Developmental changes in memorization processes." *Cognitive Psychology*, 1, 324-340.

Fusco, E., & Fountain, G. (1992). Reflective teacher, Reflective learner. In A. L. Costa, J. A. Bellanca, & R. Fogarty (Eds.), *If minds matters: A foreword to the future*, Volume 1 (pp. 239-255). Palatine, IL: IRI/Skylight Publishing.

Hattie, J., Bibbs, J., & Purdie, N. (1996). "Effects of learning skills interventions on student learning: A meta-analysis." *Review of Educational Research*, 66(2), 99-136.

Lyon, T. D., & Flavell, J. F. (1993). "Young children's understanding of forgetting over time." *Child Development*, 64(5), 789-800.

Markman, E. M.(1979). "Realizing that you don't understand: Elementary school children's awareness of inconsistencies." *Child Development*, 50, 643–655.

Marzano, R. J. (1988). *Dimensions of Thinking: A Framework for Curriculum and Instruction*. Alexandria, VA: ASCD.

Mokhtari, K., & Reichard, C. (2002). "Assessing students' metacognitive awareness of reading strategies." *Journal of Educational Psychology*, 94 (2), 249–259.

Palincsar, A. S., & Brown, D. (1981). "Enhancing instructional time through attention to metacognition." *Educational Researcher*, 10 (2:) 14–21.

Perkins, D. (1992). *Smart Schools: Better Thinking and Learning for Every Child*. New York: Free Press.

Ridley, D. S., Schutz, P. A., Glanz, R. S., & Weinstein, C. E. (1992). "Self-regulated learning: The interactive influence of metacognitive awareness and goal-setting." *Journal of Experimental Education*, 60 (4), 293-306.

Schunk, D. H. (2008). "Why this and why now? Introduction to the Special Issue on Metacognition, Self-Regulation, and Self-Regulated Learning." *Educational Psychology Review*, 20(4), 369-372.

Scruggs, T. E., Mastropieri, M. A., Monson, J., & Jorgenson, C. (1985). "Maximizing what gifted students can learn: Recent findings of learning strategy research." *Gifted Child Quarterly*, 29(4), 181-185.

Swartz, R. J., & Perkins, D. N. (1989). *Teaching Thinking: Issues and Approaches*. Pacific Grove, CA: Midwest Publications.

Tomlinson, C., & McTighe, J. (2006). *Integrating Differentiated Instruction + Understanding by Design: Connecting Content and Kids*. Alexandria, VA ASCD.

Winn, W., & Snyder D. (1996). Cognitive perspectives in psychology. In D. H. Jonassen (Ed.), *Handbook of Research for Educational Communications and Technology* (pp. 112-142). New York: Simon & Schuster Macmillan.

CHAPTER TWO

The Language of Thinking: Creating a Metacognitive Vocabulary in the Classroom

Kolencik/Hillwig

> "Language is the essential condition of knowing, the process by which experience becomes knowledge."
>
> Halliday, 1993, p. 94

This chapter examines the language that implements the teaching of thinking. It discusses verbal, written, and graphic languages that assist in thinking across disciplines to build students' thought processes in order to conduct themselves most effectively as learners. Moreover, this chapter presents the language of thinking to inspire independent learning and to create and foster the culture and community of a thoughtful classroom. To clarify the meaning of "thoughtful" classroom for this context, we refer not to disposition, but to the thinking classroom.

A number of research studies have found the teachers' use of language plays an integral role in the teaching and learning process. A teacher's choice of words, phrases, metaphors, and interaction sequences invokes thoughtful learning, thus, creating a thoughtful classroom. Because the role of language is an integral component in the teaching and learning process, the authors devoted this chapter to briefly discuss the importance of the teacher's language of thinking to foster understanding in cultivating a thoughtful classroom.

What Is the Language of Thinking?

What is the connection between metacognition and the language of thinking? If we are to teach students metacognitive processes and structures in order to become independent learners, we need to discuss the language of thinking. In creating a thoughtful classroom, we must consider

- what is said,
- how we say it
- what we are doing
- how we are doing it

The language of thinking not only helps us communicate, but it also regulates the thought processes by providing a culture of concepts to guide thinking and reflect on one's own thinking. In other words, "the discourse the mind carries on with itself," as Socrates said in *Theatetus*. The words used by the teacher in the classroom influence the way students will think about the world, including their own inner world; therefore, regulating their thoughts about learning.

The language of thinking is defined in the literature as the language we use to talk about thinking. According to Tishman and Perkins (1997), the language of thinking can be surprisingly sparse in classrooms and texts. Talking helps students learn to think. Terms such as predict, reflect, explain, classify, hypothesize, or justify are examples of words that precisely identify an intellectual process and are representative of the everyday vocabulary of thinking.

Metacognitive talk, as Marzano's (1998) research shows, is one of the most powerful tools for improving student learning. Marzano also indicates that teachers are often reluctant to use thinking terms as a subject of conversation because students would not understand. However, Marzano (1998) states that awareness and a little practice will help teachers become comfortable implementing metacognitive talk and strategies and once they begin to see the benefits, metacognitive talk will become a regular part of their instruction.

Costa (2008), urges teacher to "speak cogitare," that is, "using language to evoke thinking in others by using specific cognitive terminology rather than vague abstract terms." According to Costa (2008), when teachers use cognitive terminology to instructing students, students will be able to internalize these terms and begin to make the terms a part of their own vocabulary.

Table 2.1 cites some examples of phrases and questions teachers should use to promote metacognitive thinking.

Frequently Used Teacher Language	Metacognitive Talk: Vocabulary of Thinking
What do you think happened? support your view?	What evidence do you have to
Can you list...	How would you prioritize...?
How do you know ...?	How would you distinguish between...?
How can you explain...?	How would you justify...
What would happen if...	What do you recommend as the solution to the issue? Predict a solution
Tell me....	Convince me...
Make a map	Generate/Create a map

Table 2.1

all high order thinking verbs.

When teachers become more deliberate in the ways they formulate questions to include cognitive terms, they model the metacognitive awareness that students need to develop. Teachers who use language artfully can promote a thoughtful classroom, one in which the vocabulary of thinking frames learning. This language highlights the process of thoughtful learning and differentiates between thinking that is shallow and superficial and thinking that is deep and meaningful. Students grow as thinkers when they are asked questions that require them to justify and support their opinions instead of providing a quick, flippant response. For example, instead of asking students, Should we clone humans? We should ask, what hypothesize do you have to support cloning?

Questions such as the ones in Table 2.1 ask students to engage in understanding performances, explaining, choosing, extrapolating, and developing arguments, thus, encouraging students to think deeply and push them to higher levels of understanding. Here are examples of questions and prompts that can be asked by the teacher throughout the lesson.

USE AT THE BEGINNING OF LESSON

1. Tell what you know about _____(a new concept).
2. What is your opinion about _____ (topic of the day)?
3. Describe an experience you have had relating to _____ (topic of the day).
4. Explain how _____(topic of the day) plays a part in your life.
5. Explain how _____(topic of the day) will play a part in your life ten years from now.
6. Summarize what you have learned so far about _____(previously studied topic).
7. What has been the impact of _____(previously studied topic) on your life?
8. Describe a difficulty you have had related to _____(new or previously studied topic).
9. How do you think _____ (previously studied topic) relate to _____(new topic)?
10. List one to three questions about _____(new topic).
11. Do you think your classmates understand what's going on? Why? Why not?
12. Why is the teacher presenting this lesson?

USE IN THE MIDDLE OF THE LESSON

1. Write a question you have about anything we have discussed so far.
2. Write a sentence telling how knowing about _____(new topic) might be useful to you personally.
3. What is interfering with your learning right now?
4. How do you feel about this issue now?
5. How would you feel about this issue if you were _____(someone likely to have a different perspective)?
6. What are you thinking about right now?

7. How to you feel when you hear someone one say_____(a controversial statement about the topic of study)?

8. How do you think your best friend (or boyfriend or girlfriend) feels about _____(controversial topic)?

USE AT THE END OF A LESSON

1. How do you think your feelings about _____(new topic) is different from your teachers (or friends or parents)?
2. Summarize what you have learned today about _____(new topic).
3. Write a revised definition of _____(new concept).
4. Write a question you still have about _____(new concept).
5. Explain how _____(new topic) relates to _____(old topic).
6. How could the teacher have made this lesson easier to understand?
7. How will you use the information you learned today?
8. What went wrong with the lesson today?
9. What was good about the lesson today?

In sum, if we are to lead students to become independent learners, the culture of the thinking classroom must center around the vocabulary of thinking. To achieve thoughtful learning in the classroom that promotes and encourages metacognition, one must remember that variables such as how much the teacher models, expects, communicates, interacts, and makes time for thoughtfulness in learning are critical.

Investigating Further

Barell, J. (1995). *Teaching for thoughtfulness: Classroom strategies to enhance intellectual development.* White Plains, NY: Longman.

Costa, A. L. (2001). *Developing minds: A resource book for teaching thinking* (3rd Edition). Alexandria, VA: Association of Supervision and Curriculum Development.

Costa, A. L. (2008) *The school as a home for the mind: Creating mindful curriculum, instruction, and dialogue.* Thousand Oaks, CA: Corwin Press.

Costa, A. L. (2009). *Habits of mind across the curriculum: Practical and creative strategies for teachers.* Alexandria, VA: Association of Supervision and Curriculum Development.

REFERENCES

Appelbaum, P. M. (2000). Eight critical points for mathematics. In D. W. Weil & H. K. Anderson (Eds.), *Perspectives in critical thinking: Essays by teachers in theory and practice* (pp. 41-55). New York: Peter Lang.

Costa, A. (1991). *The school as a home for the mind.* Palatine, IL: Skylight Publishing.

Costa, A. (2008). *The school as a home for the mind: Creating mindful curriculum, instruction, and dialogue.* Thousand Oaks, CA: Corwin Press.

Halliday, M. A. (1993). "Towards a language based theory of learning." *Linguistics and Education* 5, 98-116.

Marzano, R. J. (1998). *A theory-based meta-analysis of research on instruction.* Aurora, CO: McREL. Retrieved February 21, 2010. Available www.mcrel.org/PDF/Instruction/5982RR_InstructionMeta_Analysis.pdf*

Plato. *Theateus.* In E. Hamilton & H. Cairns (Eds.), *The collected diaglogues of Plato.* Princeton, NJ: Princeton University Press, 1961, p. 190a.

Tishman, S., & Perkins, D. (1997). The language of thinking. *Kappan, 78*(5), 368-374.

Tishman, S., & Perkins, D. (1998). The language of thinking. In A. E. Woolfolk (Ed.), *Readings in educational psychology* (2nd ed.; pp. 125-132). Boston, MA: Allyn & Bacon.

SECTION TWO

Metacognitive Strategies

CHAPTER THREE

Thinking Aloud

Kolencik/Hillwig

> When the mind is thinking, it is talking to itself.
>
> Plato

This chapter concentrates on the "think aloud," one of the most common strategies associated with metacognition. This strategy calls for a cognitive monologue on behalf of the teacher and requires students to verbalize their thoughts.

What Are the Nuts and Bolts?

One of the most common strategies associated with metacognition is the think aloud. During a teacher think aloud the teacher simply shares the thinking steps followed to complete a specific task. While this appears on the surface to be a straightforward and relatively easy strategy to implement, it must be carried out with purposeful "teacher talk". The teacher think aloud is not simply vocalizing every thought that pops into one's head, but rather sharing the thinking processes that the expert (the teacher) utilizes in given situations. When implementing the think aloud, the teacher points out possible problems, misunderstandings, or "thinking errors" that the learner might have or encounter. The expert also shares the questions asked of self while working through task completion.

The aspect of the think aloud that is difficult is that the "expert" carries out thinking tasks with such automaticity that to self-analyze and vocalize each segment of the overall thinking process and associated tasks takes a great deal of consideration and practice. The think aloud offers teachers an opportunity to verbally share various thinking strategies that are necessary to solve problems, improve understanding and how and when to implement appropriate strategies.

Rutherford, in her work, *Why Didn't I Learn This in College* (2002), states the need for the teacher think aloud quite succinctly. She indicates that "our students think that we were born" being able to do many of the cognitive tasks that they see us accomplish. She further indicates that when we are modeling or demonstrating, we often don't share the problems that we've encountered along the way to becoming proficient.

A teacher think aloud can be as simple as thinking aloud the steps one would follow in decoding an unfamiliar word to something as complex as analyzing Lincoln's Gettysburg address. The teacher think aloud is appropriate for all grade levels, most types of learners, and all disciplines.

The think aloud can and should be used in conjunction with other metacognitive strategies. The think aloud can effectively convey how to implement self-monitoring strategies, utilization of mnemonic devices, and the support provided by graphic organizers. When the teacher provides a think aloud accompanying the other metacognitive strategies, the opportunity for student success is increased. Likewise, the teacher think aloud provides an opportunity to integrate other researched-based strategies into the instructional repertoire. For example, Marzano's work, *Classroom Instruction that Works* (2001), includes, but is not limited to, identifying similarities and differences and summarizing techniques. These strategies lend themselves well to the teacher think aloud. Specific examples of the integration of these strategies will be provided later in the chapter.

Simply stated, when providing a teacher think aloud the teacher should employ the following:

- Describe what is going on in one's mind while thinking.
- Model the process first for students before directing them to do so
- Provide an opportunity for the students to practice in pairs or cooperative learning groups until comfortable with the process in a large group setting

What Does the Research Say?

The literature strongly supports the teacher think aloud as one of the primary building blocks to students' success in all disciplines and at all levels of learning.

- Think alouds are effective as directed reading-thinking activities in teaching the skills of comprehension monitoring (Baumann, Seifert-Kessell, & Jones, 1993).
- Think alouds are effective as a diagnostic tool to assess students' abilities to use inferences as they read (Laing & Kamhi, 2002).
- Students who verbalize their thoughts while reading score significantly higher on comprehension tests (Anderson & Roit, 1993).
- Think alouds use a modeling technique to help students improve their comprehension (Davey, 1983).
- Modeling, when applied to metacognition, "seeks to help students recognize that people who successfully think about challenging topics carefully monitor their own thinking processes" (Savage et al., 2006, p. 260).
- Execution and explanation are critical to the success of modeling and that one without the other is insufficient. The teacher think aloud is a perfect example of modeling with both execution and explanation (Walberg et al., 1992).
- Teachers who spend more time demonstrating and explaining procedures and skills are more effective than teachers who spend less time doing so (Rosenshine, 1985).
- Good modeling not only includes explaining the expected outcomes and demonstrating steps to be taken, but teaching those steps and thinking aloud to illustrate the thinking that takes place at each step of the process (Silver, Strong, & Perini, 2007).
- Effective problem solvers subvocalize (talk to themselves), restate the situation, recheck progress, and evaluate whether or not thinking

is moving in an appropriate direction.... These steps support students thinking of their own thinking and being able to verbalize their thought (Orlich et al., 2007).

The "Think Aloud" in the Classroom

MODEL

Modeling the think aloud can be as simple or complex as appropriate for the developmental level of the learners. The authors provide examples of modeling the think aloud as a framework and springboard for the reader. It is impossible to provide examples to encompass all possible classroom scenarios and for this reason, representative exemplars are presented.

SCENARIO 1

Ms. Jones is a first grade teacher using a think aloud to support her students with decoding unknown words.

"I'm looking at this new word, b-a-i-t. I know that when I have had to decode words in the past, I thought about the phonics rules that I know. I know that when I see 2 vowels together the first vowel has usually had the long sound and that the second vowel is usually silent. Since that has helped me in the past, I'm going to try that with this word. /b/-a-/t/. Now that I sounded out the word, I know that I need to see if the word will make sense in the sentence. So I'm thinking that I know that a fisherman uses bait and not bat. Because of what I already know, it helps me to be able to figure out words that maybe I haven't read before. I had to think about the phonics rules that I know and I had to think about whether or not the word would make sense in my sentence."

SCENARIO 2

Mr. Smith is a fourth grade teacher using a think aloud to support his students with problem solving in math class. During the think aloud, Mr. Smith would not only be verbalizing his thoughts, but also would be recording equations and solutions on the whiteboard, interactive whiteboard, chalkboard, etc.

Juan and three of his friends have decided to host an after-school party for some of their friends. Juan's mother said that they can have a total of 10 people for the party at his house. They want to have pizza and fruit punch for the party. They need to determine how many people they can invite and how much money each will need to contribute for the refreshments. They want each person to be able to have 2 pieces of pizza and 2 8 ounce glasses of punch. The chart below shows the cost associated with the punch and pizza. Solve the problem and state how many people they will invite, how many pizzas they will need to purchase along with how much punch they need to buy. What will the total cost of the refreshments be and how much will each friend need to contribute?

8-slice Pizza	One 40-ounce bottle of punch
$6.00	$3.90

"I'm thinking about this word problem and remembering the things that have helped me in the past when I had to do a similar type of problem. I know that the first thing that I need to do is to read the problem and make sure that I know exactly what I'm being asked to do. I also know that sometimes there is information that is important and sometimes there is information that isn't necessary, so I'm going to read the problem again and I know that it helps me to highlight the important information. That way I will focus my attention on the important facts and disregard the information that won't help me solve the problem. I'm going to go back and re-read the problem aloud because I know that it helps me to better understand the problem if I see it and hear it." (Mr. Smith reads the problem aloud.) "Now I want to highlight the information that I think is important. I think that it's important that Juan's mother said that there can be a total of 10 people, so I'm going to highlight that. It's important to know that each person will have 2 pieces of pizza and 2 eight ounce glasses of punch, so I'll highlight that too. I'm thinking that I need to look at the chart and see how much the items cost that I need to buy. I think it's important that I highlight the cost of each of these items. I'm also thinking that this problem is asking me to find out more than one thing, so I need to make sure that I answer all of the questions being asked here. I'm going to look back at the problem and find out what the problems asks me to find first. When I go back to the problem it says that they can have 10 people, but I don't think that they can invite 10 people because that would be too many. I know that it says Juan and 3 of his friends want to host the party, so I need to figure out how many they can invite. What I need to find out is the difference between the total number allowed, 10, and the number of people that I already know, 4. I got the

4 because Juan and 3 friends make 4 people. I know that when I want to find the difference I need to subtract and I'll do that now. 10-4=6, so Juan and his friends can invite 6 people."

Juan + 3 friends = 4 people
10 people allowed – 4 = 6 people to invite

"Now that I know that, I need to think about what is asked next and that is how much food and drinks will be needed. If 10 people are each going to have 2 pieces of pizza, a total of 20 pieces are needed."

2 pieces of pizza for each X 10 people = 20 pieces needed in all

"When I think about the drinks, I need to think about more though, because each person will have 2 8 ounce glasses of punch. I'm thinking that each person will have 16 ounces of punch because 2 times 8 equals 16 and there are 10 people total, so 10 people x16 ounces equal 160 ounces. I was thinking that when I multiply by 10 I just need to add a zero in the one's place."

2 X 8 ounces = 16 ounces
16 ounces X 10 people = 160 ounces

"Now I know that I need a total of 20 pieces of pizza and 160 ounces of punch. I'm thinking that I need to go back to the chart and figure out how many of each they need to buy. The chart says the pizzas are 8 slices each and the punch is sold in 40 ounce bottles. I know that they need 20 slices of pizza, so I'm thinking that they need to buy more than one pizza. I'm wondering how I can best determine how many pizzas they need to buy. I'm thinking that dividing the total number that they need by the number in one pizza would be one way to solve this part. So if I divide 20 / 8 the answer would be 2 with a remainder of 4."

20 slices needed / 8 slices in one pizza = 2 with a remainder of 4

"This makes me think that 2 pizzas won't be enough. I'm thinking that it is better to buy 3 pizzas and have some left over than to buy 2 pizzas and not have enough for everyone. I think that I can check my thinking with repeated addition. One pizza would be 8 slices, 2 pizzas would be 16 slices because 8+8 is 16 and 3 pizzas would be 24 pieces. Three pizzas would be the number that they would need to buy."

---

8 + 8 + 8 = 24

"Now I know that they need to buy 3 pizzas. I need to solve to find out how many bottles of punch will need to be purchased. I know that they need a total of 160 ounces. The chart says that the bottles are 40 ounces each. I'm thinking of a way to figure out how many bottles will be needed. I think that I could divide again. 160 ounces needed divided by 40 ounces in each bottle should tell me how many bottles they will need to buy."

---

160 ounces needed / 40 ounces in each bottle = 4 bottles needed

---

'I know now that they need to buy 3 pizzas and 4 bottles of punch. When I look at the chart I can see how much 1 pizza and 1 bottle of punch cost, so I'm thinking about what I need to do next to find out what the total cost will be for the party. I know I need to multiply the cost of 1 pizza by the number of pizzas needed and the cost of 1 bottle of punch by the number of bottles needed."

$6.00 X 3 pizzas = $18.00

$3.90 X 4 bottles = $15.60

"Now that I know the total cost for each item, I need to find out what the cost is all together. In order to do that I think that adding will be the best way."

$18.00 + 15.60 = $33.60

"Because I know the total cost is being shared between all 4 friends, I think that division is the way that I want to solve this part of the problem."

$33.60/4=$8.40 each friend's share

"When I've completed all of these calculations, I know that I need to make sure that I answered all of the questions asked in the problem, so I'm going to go back to the problem and re-read to make sure that I didn't leave anything out." (Mr. Smith would read aloud and point out that each answer has been determined while reading the problem.)

"I am going to list all of the answers that were asked for in the problem."

---

6 people will be invited to the party

3 pizzas need to be purchased

4 bottles of punch will be bought

The cost of the pizza and punch altogether is $33.60 and each friend's share is $8.40.

SCENARIO 3

With older students, an example of a think aloud could be analyzing a portion of Lincoln's Gettysburg Address or lines from the "Pledge of Allegiance". These are examples of writings of which the students are knowledgeable, but in many cases, haven't really given thought to the meaning. A teacher think aloud in these cases, not only provides modeling for thinking through something to increase comprehension, but can serve as a springboard for further learning tasks. (See Engagement)

> *"Four score and seven years ago, our fathers brought forth upon this continent a new nation: conceived in liberty, and dedicated to the proposition that all men are created equal."*

The teacher think aloud modeling in this scenario could look something like this:

"Today I want to begin working with Lincoln's famous Gettysburg Address that was given in 1863. I'm going to begin our work by sharing aloud my thinking through the first part of this famous work. When I begin to read and think about this, the first thing that I read is, *"Four score and seven years ago."* I'm thinking that I need to figure out what this means and I'm going to use what I already know. I know that a score is usually found in some sort of a competition, but I know that this speech was given on a battlefield, so I don't think that this is the score that I know. I'm going to look this word up to see if there is another meaning. (Here the teacher actually looks up the word.) The dictionary says that a score can be twenty people or things, along with other definitions, but I think that this one might make the most sense. So if a score is twenty, then four score and seven years ago must mean 80 and 7 more, or 87. I know that if one score is twenty then four must be four times 20 or eighty. So I'm thinking that Abe Lincoln is talking about something that happened 87 years ago. Next he said, *"Our fathers brought forth upon this continent a new nation..."* I know that our forefathers are the people that came before us, so I think that Lincoln must have been talking about the people that were here ahead of us when he said "our fathers". When he talks about this continent I am thinking that he meant North America because Gettysburg is in Pennsylvania and Pennsylvania is in North America. He also said that they brought forth a new nation. I know that the speech was given in 1863 and I have already figured out that he said this happened 87 years ago. I'm thinking that if I subtract 87 from 1863, I can find out the year that he was talking about in the speech. When I do that my answer is 1776. I know that is an important year in our nation's history. Lincoln was actually talking about our country being started in 1776. Now, I want to think about what the next part of that line means.

"...conceived in liberty, and dedicated to the proposition that all men are created equal."

I know that conceived means started and liberty is another word for freedom. When I read the rest of that sentence, I'm using context clues to determine that it means dedicated to the idea that everyone is equal. I think that Abraham Lincoln was actually saying that in 1776 the people that were here before us started our country with the idea that all people were equal."

The steps in scenario 1 are far simpler than the steps in scenarios 2 and 3 because the tasks in the second and third scenarios are far more complex. The important thing to note is that the teacher actually thinks out loud while modeling and solving the problem. It involves detailed, step-by-step verbalizing. The teacher is actually sharing with the students the thought processes involved in completing the task.

When modeling the think aloud, the teacher must verbalize things like looking for patterns, finding similarities and differences, summarizing, indentifying what is known and unknown (Orlich, 2007) and self-monitoring. In other words, are my actions and thoughts moving toward the desired outcome? Through hearing and practicing these strategies, students move toward becoming independent, strategic learners.

Teachers must also help students develop self-questioning skills to use with the thinking. Questions such as:

"Have I seen this or something like this before?"
"Does this make sense?"
"Do I understand the vocabulary?"
"Are there any patterns here?"
"Can I find any similarities or differences?"

These aren't questions that students will come up with on their own. Teachers must support the development of the self-questioning skills and the think aloud is one strategy that will assist with this development. We will now look at how engagement would look as the next step.

Engage

Once the teacher has worked through the actual think aloud with the students, an opportunity for engagement should be presented. This engagement could first be framed as prompting followed by probing questions. Let's explore what engagement might look like with Scenario 1.

In this example, Ms. Jones provided a think aloud dealing with decoding. An appropriate form of follow-up and engagement could take the form of scenario such as this.

"Please look at the word that is underlined in the sentence written on the board."
THE GOAT EATS OATS.
"Think about what you know already regarding decoding words and plan to tell your study partner what you are thinking. I'm going to give you 30 seconds to think."

After providing the specified "think time", the teacher then follows with:

> "You now have 60 seconds to think aloud with your study partner. Each of you is required to share something with your partner that you were thinking about decoding the underlined word."

When the 60-second sharing time is up, ask if there is a volunteer willing to share what he or she was thinking. This is a variation of Lyman's (1981) "Think, Pair, Share" strategy (Guillaume et al., 2007). Since the teacher provided a think aloud with the decoding strategy prior to the "Think, Pair, Share", it would not be uncommon for students to emulate the thinking and language of learning previously stated by the teacher.

Engagement would be further developed by asking students to think about the complete sentence and be prepared to think aloud to complete the following sentence frame.

> When I look at the sentence, I'm thinking that _____.

Representative responses could include:

> When I look at the sentence, I'm thinking that goat makes sense and got doesn't.
> When I look at the sentence, I'm thinking that oats would follow the same phonics rule as goat.
> When I look at the sentence, I'm thinking that eats will probably have a long e sound because it has two vowels together.
> Probing questions would spark further opportunities for thinking aloud.
> When I look at the sentence, I'm thinking that goat makes sense and got doesn't. (Why do you think that the underlined word is goat and not got?)
> When I look at the sentence, I'm thinking that oats would follow the same phonics rule as goat. (What do you already know that helped you to think that oats would follow the same phonics rule?)
> When I look at the sentence, I'm thinking that eats will probably have a long e sound because it has two vowels together. (Can you think of another time when used this phonics rule to help

you decode an unfamiliar word?)

Scenario 2 offers several opportunities for engagement. Teacher questioning to promote engagement might look something like this:

* Do you think that there are other key terms or phrases that you would have highlighted? What are they and tell us what you are thinking about that indicates they're important.
* When you have worked with problems like this in the past, what strategies did you use that helped you solve the problem?
* Think about a different way that the problem could have been solved and share it with your study partner.

Further tasks with Scenario 3 might include rewriting a portion of familiar song lyrics in the students' own words, or with a study partner presenting their own version of the "Pledge of Allegiance", for example, that conveys the same meaning, but in the students' own words.

Begin the engagement portion of the strategy in a non-threatening environment for the students. The teacher needs to have established a learning climate where students are willing to take risks and feel comfortable sharing their thoughts. Initially, provide the opportunity for the students to work with a study partner in a "Think, Pair, Share" activity where the students only need to do the think aloud with their partners. After several opportunities to practice the think aloud in the small group setting, ask for volunteers to share their thinking with the entire group. For some students, it may take longer for them to feel comfortable enough to share with the whole group.

Engagement can be encouraged using photographs or illustrations as discussed in the following example.

Figure 3.1 Microsoft Office Clip Art

What do you know by looking at this picture?
Prompting questions could include:

"What season is it?
"What time of the day is it?"
"What is the setting of the picture?"
"What kind of business do these people have?"
"What do you already know that you are using to help formulate
your ideas?"

The use of a graphic organizer could also support students and help them
organize their thinking. Something as simple as Table 3.1 could be used.

Sample Graphic Organizer

What are you thinking?	Why?	What do you know?	How did this help you?

Table 3.1 Sample Graphic Organizer

Transfer

Transfer in this section will deal with both the teacher and the student. For the teacher, the graphic organizer provided will assist in the "behind the scenes" work for the teacher think aloud. As one might employ the Big 6 (Eisenberg & Berkowitz, 1987) for problem solving, the authors suggest the 3 P's for the teacher think aloud. Planning, preparation, and presentation are represented by the 3 P's. First, the teacher must plan where the think aloud will be used in instruction. Next, preparation involves thinking about every detail and aspect of his or her own thinking that will be shared aloud to support the students' development of metacognitive skills. Finally, the teacher presents the think aloud integrated into classroom instruction.

The 3 P's of Think Aloud

Plan	Prepare	Present
Where will I use the Think Aloud Strategy?	What aspects of my thinking must I convey to my students?	After conducting the Think Aloud, reflect on the presentation and assess your implementation.
	What details should I include?	Did you include all aspects that you intended?
		Should you have prepared for something that you hadn't anticipated?
		How will you prepare differently in the future for use of this strategy?

Providing students an opportunity to develop their own metacognitive thinking is the goal with the think aloud strategy. The insightful teacher will capitalize on each and every opportunity to draw the student into this type of in-depth thinking. The simple questions of, "What are you thinking right now?" and "Why?" are good starting points to bring the students toward automaticity with the self-monitoring strategies integrated into the think aloud. Along with this self-monitoring comes transfer, where students will apply the strategy to various aspects of their academic and personal lives. Graphic organizers can support students in acquiring and developing the thinking skills desired. One such graphic organizer suggested is the "Think, Pair, Share."

Think	Pair	Share
Record your ideas.

Remember to think about times that you've used this strategy in the past or have seen similarities or differences. | Record one or more idea/s you and your partner discussed.

Remember to share your "thinking" with your partner. How did you come up with your conclusion? This should be part of your discussion. | Record something interesting you heard during the group sharing.

Jot down things shared by the group members that you or your partner hadn't discussed. Did you hear something that you will use in the future when faced with a similar task? |

The use of a Venn diagram can assist with a think aloud when working with similarities and differences. While thinking aloud through discriminating between similarities and differences between 2 or more items, ideas, or concepts, the teacher provides the visual support in the form of the Venn diagram. The Venn diagram is a very commonly used metacognitive tool and aligns perfectly with the idea of transfer. The column Venn diagram presented is a variation of a Column Venn diagram available at http://www.freeology.com.

Column Venn Diagram

List the distinguishing or different characteristics for each issue in the outer columns and similar or shared characteristics in the middle column.

Issue 1	Similar or Shared Characteristics of Each	Issue 2

Assess

Assessment in the think aloud realm should be considered in two areas. First, the teacher must do some self-assessment when conducting the think aloud. Teacher reflection should include the following self-questioning:

1. Was the think aloud structured with purposeful talk leading to the outcome I desired for my students?
2. Did the think aloud cover all of my thinking with this scenario?
3. Did I leave out any important thought processes that the students need to know? Did I assume that they would know things and not verbalize them?

These are important questions for self-assessment of the teacher think aloud.

Next, the assessment of the students' think aloud should be formative. In most cases, one would not assess for evaluation or grading purposes. Teacher observation and keeping running records could be one effective means of assessing the students' development of the think aloud strategy.

It should be noted that the think aloud is most commonly considered in the realm of instruction; however, when applied by the student, it demonstrates that the student is not only cognizant of his or her own thinking, but is also able to verbalize it.

Classroom Snapshot: On Your Own

Reflect on what you now know regarding thinking aloud and record how this will look in your classroom.

1. What is a think aloud?
2. Why should I use a think aloud?
3. How would I use a think aloud?
4. How can I integrate think alouds into my lessons to engage students' metacognitive skills?

Investigating Further

PRINT

Oster, L. (2001). "Using the think-aloud for reading instruction." *The Reading Teacher*, 55(1), 64-69.

Oster discusses the procedures teachers use to model think-aloud strategies and describes how the think-aloud is used as a metacognitive strategy. Also includes information on using the think-aloud as an assessment tool.

Wade, S. E. (1990). "Using think alouds to assess comprehension." *The Reading Teacher*, 43(7), 442-451.

This article describes ways to use think aloud strategies to assess how well a student comprehends what is being read and gives information about how to use think alouds as an assessment tool.

Wilhelm, J. D. (2001). *Improving Comprehension with Think-Aloud Strategies*. New York: Scholastic Inc.

A collection of guidelines, checklists, and assessment tools to start think-aloud strategies with your students

Web Resources

HOT CHALK

http://www.hotchalk.com/mydesk/index.php/editorial/121-classroom-best-practices/63-developing-teacher-think-alouds

Provides details on developing a teacher think aloud; also presents information on creating a digital think aloud

INTERACTIVE THINK ALOUDS

http://teacher.scholastic.com/products/scholasticprofessional/pdfs/Interactive_Think-Aloud_Lessons_sample1.pdf

Offers 25 interactive lessons on think alouds to increase your students' learning engagement

EFFECTIVE TEACHING

http://www.tantasqua.org/superintendent/Profdevelopment/etthinkalouds.html

An overview of the think aloud; examples of How to use think-alouds in science, social studies, and math; includes a Think-Aloud Assessment

REFERENCES

Baumann, J.F., Jones, L.A., & Seifert-Kessell, N. (1993, November). "Using think alouds to enhance children's comprehension monitoring abilities." *The Reading Teacher,* 47(3), 184-193.

Davey, B. (1983, October). "Think aloud: Modeling the cognitive processes of reading comprehension." *Journal of Reading,* 44-47.

Eggan, P. D., & Kauchak, D. P. (2006). *Strategies and models for teachers: Teaching content and thinking skills.* Boston, MA: Pearson Allyn Bacon.

Eisenberg, M., & Berkowitz, R. E. (1987). *The Big 6 Skills Approach.* Available http://www.big6.com/.

Guillaume, A.M., Yopp, R. H., & Yopp, H.K. (2007). *50 strategies for active learning.* Upper Saddle River, NJ: Pearson Merrill Prentice Hall.

Hunter, M. (1982). *Mastery teaching.* El Segundo, CA: TIP Publications.

Laing, S. P., & Kamhi, A. G. (2002, September). "The use of think-aloud protocols to compare inferencing abilities in average and below-average readers." *Journal of Learning Disabilities,* 437-448.

Marzano, R. J., Pickering, D. J., & Pollock, J. E. (2001). *Classroom instruction that works: Research-based strategies for increasing student achievement.* Alexandria, VA: ASCD.

Orlich, D. C, Harder, R. J., Callahan, R. C., Trevisan, M. S., & Brown, A. H. (2007). *Teaching strategies: A guide to effective instruction.* Boston, MA: Houghton Mifflin.

Rutherford, P. (2002). *Why didn't I learn this in college?: Teaching and learning in the 21st century.* Alexandria, VA: Just ASK Publications.

Silver, H. F., Strong, R.W., & Perini, M. J. (2007). *The strategic teacher: Selecting the right research-based strategy for every lesson.* Upper Saddle River, NJ: Pearson Merrill Prentice Hall.

Savage, T., Savage, M., & Armstrong, D. (2006). *Teaching in the secondary school.* Upper Saddle River, NJ: Pearson Merrill Prentice Hall.

Someren, W. M., Barnard, F. Y., & Sandberg, A. C. (1994). *The think aloud method. A practical guide to modeling cognitive process.* London: Harcourt Brace.

Walberg, H. J. et al. (1992). *Teaching for thinking.* Reston, VA: NASSP.

CHAPTER FOUR

Thinking Journals

Kolencik/Hillwig

"We write and read in order to know each other's responses, to connect ourselves more fully with the human world, and to strengthen the habit of truth-telling in our midst."

DeMott, 1990, p. 6

This chapter tackles the use of journals for assessing the reflectiveness of students' responses, evidence of transfer to other classes or life outside of school, and students' ability to plan, monitor, and self-evaluate.

What Are the Nuts and Bolts?

The thinking journal is a fundamental tool to jump-start developing metacognitive skills because it is essentially a vehicle based on the writer's processes of reflection. Journaling provides an avenue for students to recognize as well as reflect on how they think, thus, making it an active learning tool. Journal writing affords students with the opportunity to explore, question, connect, choose, and persist. It is a constructivist approach that enables students to reflect and connect, to construct their understanding of the world, to become conscious of what, and, more importantly, of how they have learned. Journal writing provides students with an arena in which they can capture their first response or reaction to the material presented. This is a critical step toward reflective analysis in the metacognitive process. Moreover, the thinking journal causes students to focus their attention and helps them to know whether or not they understand something. If they cannot explain it, they probably cannot understand it. Along the same lines, being asked to write the explanation of something can encourage a deeper approach to learning.

Likewise, journal writing serves a number of purposes:
- to record experience
- to facilitate learning from experience
- to support understanding and the representation of the understanding
- to develop critical thinking and an questioning attitude
- to encourage metacognition
- to increase active involvement in and ownership in learning
- to increase ability in reflection and thinking
- to enhance problem-solving skills
- to promote self-empowerment as a means of self-expression
- to enhance creativity
- to improve writing
- to foster communication whether individually, between or interaction within another or in a group
- to encourage exploration and risk-taking by the students as well as to teach content.

A thinking journal can take on a variety of formats: unstructured formats such as free writing or structured forms such as double entry journals or dialogue journals. Research by Costa, Bellanca, and Fogarty (1992) recommend using thinking journals on a regular basis in the following ways:
- to record key ideas from a lecture, movie, presentation, field trip, or reading assignment
- to make predictions about what will happen next in a story, movie, experiment, school, or national or world event
- to record questions
- to summarize the main ideas of a book, movie, lecture, or reading

- to reflect on the information presented
- to connect the ideas presented to other subject areas or to the student's personal life
- to monitor change in an experiment or event over time
- to respond to questions posted by the teacher or other students
- to brainstorm ideas about potential projects, papers, or presentations
- to help identify problems
- to record problem-solving techniques
- to keep track of the number of problems solved, books read, or homework assignments completed.

Additionally, keep in mind that writing and drawing are parallel enterprises. You may want to consider having students draw pictures or construct concept maps as part of their thinking journals as well.

As stated earlier, journaling provides an important outlet for students' feelings and perceptions; however, at times, students need a bit of guidance and prompting to begin to write and to overcome being intimidated by "the blank page." The following similes can be used to help students understand the journal writing process.

- Think of your journal as a letter to yourself. What would you like yourself to know? What would you want to remember five years from now? Ten years from now. Turn your journal into a dialogue with yourself. Argue, debate, reconcile.
- Think of your journal as a snapshot album and yourself as a roving photographer clicking a shutter on life. Include "light and dark" contrasts, color, texture, portraits and landscapes. See life though various lenses: microscopic, wide-angle, and close-up.
- Think of your journal as a giant wardrobe into which you can step to try on marvelous clothes. Imagine being someone in another country in native dress. Be rich or poor. Be who you want to be. Look in the mirror and see how you look. What do you see? How do you feel? What will you do in your new persona. Try writing just phrases that rhyme or maybe a poem.

- Think of your journal as your MP3 recorder attached directly to your brain. Record your stream-of-consciousness thoughts. Don't fuss for words, write as fast as you can think, using dashes or dots.
- Think of your journal as a jewelry box full of precious gems and stones. Write an idea, epigram, cleaver phrase, pun, or words of wisdom on each gem. Describe how you pick each gem or stone to associate with your words.
- Think of your journal as a history memoirs and yourself as a VIP: the average citizen. Write to an extraterrestrial reader or a terrestrial reader in the 22nd century. Let him or her know how we lived and thought.
- Think of your journal as a travelogue. You have just arrived from another planet. Record the quaint customs, lore, speech patterns, superstitions, and other sights and bits of culture of your terrain. Write what you observe. Put yourself in others' minds, especially people whom you dislike or who seem foreign to you. Tell others what you believe.

In sum, journal writing is a powerful and revealing active learning tool that provides great opportunities for learning, understanding, and clarifying students' thought processes.

What Does the Research Say?

Findings from the published literature strongly support the use of journal writing as a metacognitive strategy.
- The use of dialogue journal, or "written conversation," unites talk and writing in a functional, interactive way (Staton, 1988).
- Teaching students to use writing to organize their ideas about what they are reading is a proven procedure that enhances comprehension for text (National Reading Panel, 2000).
- Students should be encouraged to talk and write their ideas, to understand the underlying concepts being taught and to put those concepts in to their own words (Kohn, 1999).
- Writing down what is presented, observed, or thought about

assists the brain in organizing and making sense of very complicated, multifaceted pieces of information (Jensen, 2000).

- It is one thing for students to succeed in writing good essays when teachers tell them what to write about; it is another for students to come up with original ideas for stories (Sternberg & Grigorenko, 2000).

- Writing journals, newspaper articles, editorials, essays, posters, or short stories are examples of ways to access emotional memories (Sprenger, 1999).

- Journal writing...allows one to recognize, in writing, the natural thought processes (Wetherell & Mullins, 1996).

- Writing about the solving of a problem improves the process of problem solving (Selfe & Arbabi, 1986).

- Journal writing sets up a self-provided feedback system (Yinger, 1985).

- Writing can record a train of thought and relate it in past, present, and future (Emig, 1977).

- Journal writing has been associated with improved capacities for metacognition (McCrindle & Christensen,1995).

The Thinking Journal in the Classroom

MODEL

When modeling the use of journals to develop metacognition, the teacher must stress reflection, self-assessment, and disposition for one's own ability to be successful with the task at hand (Ben-Hur, 2006). Tomlinson and McTighe (2006) state that effective learners are "mindful of how they learn." The thinking journal serves as an excellent vehicle for developing "mindful" learners. Ben-Hur (2006) addresses the use of journals specifically in math and states the following:

Students should be encouraged to use in their journals language such as the following:

"This was possible because ... Alternatively ..."
"The problem here, I believe, was that ..."
"While it may be true that ..."
"On the one hand ..."

"In thinking back ..."

"On reflection ..."

"I guess that this problem has made me aware of ..."

While Ben-Hur (2006) was writing for math, it should be noted that the prompts presented could easily be adapted for use in most content areas. The teacher must be certain that the purpose for the thinking journal has been presented in a clear and concise manner. Students must see that the thinking journal is a vehicle for them to organize, summarize and verbalize (in writing) their own thinking. It presents the opportunity for the students to reflect, but also to be able to revisit their thinking over time. Students when reviewing previous thinking journal entries are able to monitor their own metacognitive growth. The students must be encouraged to reflect and write on all aspects of their thinking. They must constantly be prompted to ask themselves, "Why?" Why did this work? Why will this help me? Why should I remember this? Why should I use this again? Why should this be included in my summary?

As with any modeling, the teacher must actually explain and demonstrate how the thinking journal should be completed. This modeling would include a think aloud (chapter 3) that results in the teacher actually writing a thinking journal for the students to observe. Using the think aloud examples provided in chapter 3, let's look at how the thinking journal may come into play in the respective classrooms.

Since Ms. Jones was working with first grade students on decoding, the journaling expectations for this age group will be age appropriate. Ms. Jones could use sentence frames for her students to assist them in completing journal entries on decoding. Example journal prompts could look something like the following:

- I will remember this about decoding because _____.
- The thing I like best about this is_____ because _____.
- The part that is the easiest for me to remember is _____ because _____.
- The part that is the hardest for me to remember is _____ because_____.
- The things that I will use again when I sound out words are _____.

Ms. Jones would model her own thinking journal. She would state to her students this type of example:

"Now that I've thought through the decoding of this unknown word, I want summarize my thinking in a thinking journal. To help me organize my thoughts for my journal I'm going to use these sentence frames. (The sentence frames could be shown on a poster, whiteboard, chalkboard, or any display area that the teacher chooses.) The first frame is: *I will remember this about decoding because* _____ and I'm going to write this ending; *lots of words have 2 vowels in them.* I know this because when I read I see a lot of words like that. The next frame that I'm going to finish is, '*The thing that I like the best about this is that I think I'll be able to use it with other words when I read because I will always find words that I don't know.*"

Ms. Jones would continue modeling her thinking journal through all of the sentence frames. Once students have become comfortable with the frames provided, different and more complex sentence prompts should be given. During the second half of first grade, most students would be able to complete a simple thinking journal entry without the scaffolding of the sentence frame. Teachers will need to observe and assess when their own students would be able to complete this without the support of the framework.

In the previous sentence frames the teacher is supporting the students' metacognition by prompting them to self-monitor. Due to the young age of the students, this is an appropriate way to begin the metacognitive monologue for them. The students not only need to identify what they liked best, was easiest, hardest, etc., but they also state why. This step requires them to think about their own thinking.

In the scenario with Mr. Smith and his fourth graders solving the multi-step math problem, the thinking journal can be more independent. When modeling the thinking journal for older students, the teacher could discuss the types of things to be included in the journal entries and actually write one with the students. The teacher would state the problem-solving strategies used to solve the problem, the attitude and feelings that he (Mr. Smith) had when he solved the problem successfully, and how he felt when he first read the problem. A rubric or checklist should be introduced in order to support the students when they reach the point of completing the thinking journal independently. Modeling the use of the rubric or worksheet is important to aid the students' understanding that thinking journals require purposeful writing.

Many students will have experienced journal writing in which they write on a topic of choice, or write in a more creative mode. The thinking journal is purposeful, targeted writing. Using a rubric or checklist will guide the students toward completion of the task with the necessary reflection and self-monitoring.

An excerpt of Mr. Smith's modeling of the thinking journal follows:

"Today we're going to revisit the problem that we solved dealing with Juan and his friends planning the after school party. I'm going to share some of my thinking journal entries that I want to include for this problem solving activity. When I begin my thinking journal, I want to include what I was thinking about as I solved that problem. Now I'll begin. (At this point, Mr. Smith is actually writing and saying aloud what he is writing.)

When I first read the problem, I thought that there were a lot of things that the problem was asking me. I thought that this problem was going to be hard to solve. I went back and read the problem again so that I would know exactly what I was being asked to find out. I also highlighted important words and key phrases. Highlighting helps me to focus on the information that is important. This is something that I know helps me and I want to do that again when I have a problem like this to solve or when I'm reading something important. I know that I also broke the problem up into chunks in my mind and I solved them one at a time. Sometimes it helps me to actually draw a diagram of how I want to go about solving the problem...

Let's look at what Mr. Smith was actually doing. He shared strategies that he used to solve the problems. He wrote about doing things that he knew helped in the past and that he would probably want to use in the future. Mr. Smith also mentioned that he thought the problem would be hard when he first read it. If we would have been able to read to the conclusion of his thinking journal, we would have seen that Mr. Smith felt a sense of accomplishment by using his strategies to successfully solve the problem. The disposition for learning is important to include when modeling for students.

Mr. Smith would further state for his students that he will compare his thinking journal to the checklist to see if he included all of the important parts of a thinking journal. If he sees that he didn't address something included in the checklist, he then models how that should be included.

Thinking Journal Checklist

Did I discuss each of these areas in my thinking journal?

I understand about_____.
The strategies that I used are _____.
The strategies that will help me in other learning areas are.
I show what I already knew, what I learned and what I still want to learn more about. (K-W-L)
I am still puzzled by_____.
I might do this differently if _____.
How effective have I been in working and completing this process?
How did I reflected on my overall performance?

The think aloud example using the Gettysburg Address would be used as a springboard for modeling the thinking journal. Because the students in this scenario are assumed to be more mature learners, the teacher would model the use of the checklist and other appropriate prompting questions to serve as a catalyst for students' writing. The more mature the learner, the more complex the thinking journals should be.

Engage

Student engagement with the thinking journal comes after the teacher has modeled the strategy and explicitly described the checklist. Students are then asked to write one or two statements about their own thinking and learning. At this point, the teacher needs to provide feedback and suggest that the students refer to the prompts and checklist if they are demonstrating difficulty with the writing. Prior to beginning this process, the students should have had the opportunity to practice the think aloud with their learning partners or even possibly with the large group.

If the students are struggling with the thinking journals, start with the first prompt of the checklist and ask them to complete it in their journals.

I understand about_____.

The teacher should provide immediate verbal feedback by moving throughout the classroom and monitoring the students' work. This initial step should provide the support and scaffolding needed to help them get started and perhaps remove the obstacles that some students experience with writing. The engagement with thinking journals is writing. The teacher must provide the steps and the pacing appropriate to move his or her own students toward feeling comfortable with this type of thinking and writing.

Transfer

Transfer of the self-monitoring necessary for the thinking journal can be supported through the use of graphic organizers or thinking maps. Teachers can also encourage transfer by including probing or prompting questions in worksheets and assignments. Once the students have experienced teacher modeling of the thinking journal and have also been practicing the actual writing of the thinking journal, they can be asked to respond to "thinking journal type" questions in their daily work.

Teachers should include questions in worksheets and assignments that promote metacognition. It should become standard practice that at the end of every math, science, social studies, or literature paper, some type of prompting question will be presented. This practice will support transfer of the metacognitive strategy across the curriculum. The goal is to enable the student to self-assess and self-monitor in all academic and "real-life" situations. We must help them realize that this type of thinking is not just for the thinking journal, but that the thinking journal is to help them develop the strategic thinking that will assist them throughout their lives. Some examples of sentence starters or questions follow:

- The hardest thing about this assignment was _____.
- The thing that I learned by completing this assignment was

   _____.
- One strategy that I used in this assignment that will help with similar assignments is _____.
- How does what I learned from completing this assignment apply to my life now? How can I use this information in my life in the future? This information is important because....
- What new goal can I set because of my work on this assignment?
- Why do you think your were given this assignment?
- What have I done to help me understand or learn about this?

- I am proud of this assignment because
- One thing I am excited about is… because…

Teachers can help their students realize transfer with a simple three-column chart. Each column should be labeled with a strategy that the students have noted in their thinking journals. In each column below the strategy, instruct the students to write other areas of their academic life or out-of-school life where the strategy would help them. Table 4.1 presents an example only. Students would be able to label the columns with their own strategies and then note below where the strategies would be employed in similar situations.

Three Column Chart

I know what works best for me.	I highlight important words.	I know how long it takes me to complete a task.

Table 4.1 Three Column Chart

Assess:

The rubric provided in Table 4.2 is an excellent way for students to self-assess their thinking journals. By asking the students to complete the rubric for several of their journal entries, they can chart their own progress with the strategy. It also provides the teacher with a measure of the students' self-assessment.

When working with classes on research projects, the following research-response log in Table 4.3 could be used as a type of thinking journal at the end of each class session to have students evaluate their work habits. It functions as both a metacognitive primer and formative assessment. This journal serves several purposes: 1) Students have to account for what they've been doing; 2) students do a self-assessment of both process and content; and 3) students get to ask for help as needed, but privately. Forms should be collected at the end of each session and reviewed by the teacher. Before the next session, the teacher writes brief comment/responses to each student. The teacher can also use the results as discussion prompts for group review to address problems students may be experiencing.

Rubric for Thinking Journal Self-Assessment

Thinking Journal Behaviors	3	2	1	Score
I understand about_____.	I included details that clearly explain my understanding.	I included a few details that show my understanding.	I didn't clearly explain my understanding.	
The strategies that I used are ___.	I clearly described the strategies that I used and discussed how they helped me.	I described a few of the strategies that I used.	I didn't really describe the strategies used or how they helped me.	
These strategies will help me in other learning areas.	I clearly state other areas where these strategies will transfer and help me in the future.		I didn't really describe how these strategies will transfer and help me in the future.	
I show what I already knew, what I learned and what I still want to learn more about. (K-W-L)	I wrote about all three areas of the K-W-L.	I wrote about two areas of the K-W-L.	I wrote about one area of the K-W-L.	
I will do this differently.	I clearly and with detail explain what I would change and do differently the next time.		I didn't address what I would do differently the next time.	
I reflected on my overall performance.	I described how difficult the task was and what my strengths and weaknesses are.	I described how difficult the task was.	I didn't really address how difficult the task was.	

Comments:

Table 4.2 Rubric for Thinking Journal Self-Assessment

Research Response Log

Name:	Topic:
Focus:	Looked in:
Specific topics I have been looking for	Specific resources I used
Interesting info:	Problems I have
1-2 concepts I discovered and why this will be useful	Where/Why/How I need help

Adapted from Alice H. Yucht, **Flip It!: An Information Skills Strategy for Student Researchers (1997).**

Table 4.3 Research Response Log

This thinking journal can be used near the end of a lesson for a formative assessment. It could also be used at various intervals during the lesson so teachers can ascertain if there is confusion or misunderstanding about information.

If time permits, students then share their journals with a partner or group members. They discuss the key ideas with other students and see if they can answer each other's questions. The teacher conducts a brief discussion with the whole class to see if anyone still has questions that were not answered or that need clarification. The class then discusses the connections students made with the information and the "real-life" situations. An example can be found in Table 4.4 below:

Reflective Lesson Thinking Journal

Name: Topic:

1. Key ideas from this discussion:
2. Connections I can make with other ideas:
3. Questions I still have:

Table 4.4 Reflective Lesson Thinking Journal

Classroom Snapshot: On Your Own

Reflect on what you now know regarding thinking journals and record how this will look in your classroom.
1. What is a thinking journal?
2. Why should I use a thinking journal?
3. How would I use a thinking journal?
4. How can I integrate thinking journals into my lessons to engage students' metacognitive skills?

Investigating Further

PRINT

Edwards, P. R. (1992). Using dialectical journals to teach thinking skills. *Journal of Reading*, 35(4), 312-316.

> Step-by-step instructions of how to use dialectical journals to assist students in thinking critically. Dialectical journals allow the students to respond to text or lectures. Teachers model the simplest type of dialectical journal, which requires students to think on a literal level by restating and paraphrasing what was read or said. The teacher continues to build skills through introducing the students to thinking skills to develop more complex dialectical journals.

Fulwiler, T. (1987). *The Journal Book*. Portsmouth, NH: Boynton/Cook Publishers.

> Essays on the use of journal writing in the classroom are presented

Rainer, T. (1978). *The new diary: How to use a journal for self-guidance and expanded creativity*. New York: Tarcher/Putnam.

> Describes a list of devices to bring awareness to journal writers such as catharsis, description, free-intuitive writing, reflection, map of consciousness, guided imagery, unsent letter, altered point of view, and dialogue and tells writer how to use them.

Woodard, P. (1994). *Journal jumpstarts: Quick topics and tips for journal writing*. Fort Collins, CO: Cottonwood.

> Provides a plethora of sentences, prompts, phrases, words that can be used a catalysts for writing

WEB RESOURCES

A-Z TEACHER STUFF

http://atozteacherstuff.com/SearchEducation/Language_Arts/Writing/Journals/index.shtml

> A teacher-created site with an extensive list of ideas for journal writing topic; writing topics are searchable by grade level from first through high school.

DEVELOPING METACOGNITION

http://www.education.com/reference/article/Ref_Dev_Metacognition/

> An excellent article from ERIC discussing strategies for developing metacognitive behaviors and establishing the metacognitive environment

GOLDMINE OF JOURNAL WRITING PROMPTS

http://www.squidoo.com/journalwritingprompts

> Explore the different ways to incorporate journal writing into the classroom
>
> A collection of web links for Journal Writing Prompt Resources for all grade levels

JOURNALS IN THE CLASSROOM

http://712educators.about.com/cs/writingresources/a/journals.htm

> Journal article discussing the potential benefits of journal writing; presents information on self-understanding and clarifying thoughts and positions and student privacy.

SUPERTEACHER

http://www.superteacherworksheets.com/journal-prompts.html

> Download over one thousand journal writing topics from this site for all grade levels

WORKSHEET LIBRARY

http://www.worksheetlibrary.com/teachingtips/journalwriting.html

> K-8 journal writing prompt reproducibles

REFERENCES

Ben-Hur, M. (2006). *Concept-rich mathematics instruction: Building a strong foundation for reasoning and problem solving*. Alexandria, VA: Association for Supervision and Curriculum Development.

Costa, A. L, Bellanca, J. A., & Fogarty, R. (1992). *If minds matter: A foreword to the future, Volume 1*. Palatine, IL: IRI/Skylight Publishing.

Demott, B. (1990, March). "Why we read and write." *Educational Leadership*, 6.

Emig, J. (1977). "Writing as a model of learning." *College Composition and Communication*, 28, 122-128.

Jenson, E. (2000). "Moving with the brain in mind." *Educational Leadership*, 58(3), 34-37.

Kohn, A. (1999). *The schools our children deserve: Moving beyond traditional classrooms and tougher standards*. Boston: Houghton Mifflin.

McCrindle, A., & Christensen, C. (1995). "The impact of learning journals on metacognitive processes and learning performance." *Learning and Instruction*, 5(3), 167-185.

McTighe, J., & Wiggins, G. (2004). *The understanding by design professional development workbook*. Alexandria, VA: Association for Supervision and Curriculum Development.

National Reading Panel. (2000). *Teaching children to read*. Jessup, MD: National Institute for Literacy at EDpubs.

Selfe, C., & Arbabi, F. (1986). Writing to learn—Engineering student journals. In A. Young & T. Fulwiler (Eds.), *Writing across the disciplines*, Upper Monclair, NJ: Boynton/Cook.

Sprenger, M. (1999). *Learning and memory: The brain in action*. Alexandria, VA: Association for Supervision and Curriculum Development.

Staton, J. (1988). "An introduction to dialogue journal communication." In J. Staton et al. (Eds.) *Cognitive Views*. Norwood, NJ: Ablex.

Sternberg, R. J., & Grigorenko, E. L. (2000). *Teaching for successful intelligence: To increase student learning and acheivement*. Arlington Heights, IL: Skylight.

Tomlinson, C., & McTighe, J. (2006). *Integrating differentiated instruction and understanding by design*. Alexandria, VA: Association for Supervision and Curriculum Development.

Wetherell, J., & Mullins, G. (1996). "The use of student journals in problem-based learning." *Medical Education*, 30, 105-111.

Yinger, R. (1985). "Journal writing as a learning tool." *The Volta Review*, 87(5), 21-33.

Yucht, A. H. (1997). *Flip It!: An Information Skills Strategy for Student Researchers*. Worthington, OH: Linworth.

CHAPTER FIVE

Thinking with Mnemonics

Kolencik/Hillwig

Memory feeds imagination.

Amy Tan, U.S. novelist (1952 -)

This chapter looks at using mnemonic tools such as rhymes, acrostics, acronyms, and charting, not only to help students remember content, but also to construct, connect, and relate their thinking to content.

What Are the Nuts and Bolts?

Coming from the Greek term "mnema" meaning memory enhancing, the word "mnemonics" can be defined as a memory tool, a device, or a technique created for remembering information that is otherwise quite difficult to recall. A mnemonic can be composed of symbols, phrases, letters, sentences, or alphanumeric expressions intended to assist memory. For example, the "Thirty days has September" rhyme enables students to learn the number of days in a month or the word "homes" enables students to learn the names of the Great Lakes of the United States.

Mnemonic strategies offer a systematic approach for organizing and remembering facts that have no apparent link or connection on their own. Mnemonic devices provide the tools necessary to recall almost any type of information; thus, providing an effective pathway to jump-start learning. Mnemonics can be used to circumvent rote memorization of facts by associating the facts with prior knowledge already stored in the brain. Unfortunately, a great deal of the information students have to remember is presented as words on a printed page or on a computer screen. According to the research, the brain does not easily encode written information, thus, making it difficult to remember. Using mnemonic devices facilitates memory. The key idea is that by coding information using vivid mental images, students can reliably code both information and the structure of information, thus, using a type of metacognitive process. Mnemonic techniques work whether their two principal ingredients (recoded keywords and relating scenes) are produced either *by* or *for* a learner.

There are many different types of mnemonics. Table 5.1 lists the most common and useful mnemonics devices.

Mnemonics, though appealing, aren't magical devices, but indeed involve

Mnemonic Strategy	Definition	Example
Acronym	A word created using the first letter of each word of the important information; can also be an abbreviation formed by initial letters.	PEN=proton, electron, neutron (parts of an atom) NATO=North Atlantic Treaty Organization
Acrostic	Sentence in which the first letter of each word connects with the intended-to be- recalled information	To remember the planets: My very energetic mother just served us nine pizzas.
Chaining	Intertwine items to be remembered into a story	See Model
Keyword	Associate two items using mental imagery	See Model
Rhymes or phrases	Catchy phrase or jingle used to remember	Red sky at night, sailor's delight; red sky in morning, sailor's warning

Table 5.1 Types of Mnemonics

a metacognitive process as students create words, rhymes, or stories. The very effort of students composing and using mnemonic tools not only helps them remember content, but also engages their thought processes. According to Levin (1993), mnemonic instruction is useful for students across a wide age range, especially for students with learning disabilities.

What Does the Research Say?

The evidence of effectiveness strongly supports the use of mneumonic devices across grade levels in all curricular areas to support the metacognitive skills.

- People who use mnemonic devices learn two to three times more than those who learn normally (Markowitz & Jensen, 1999).
- Factual information can be more easily applied when mnemonic devices are used to acquire the information (Levin & Levin, 1990).
- Mnemonic tools work because they provide the brain with powerful cues for recalling chunks of information (Markowitz & Jensen, 1999).
- Mnemonics create links or associations between new information the brain is receiving and information already stored in long-term memory (Wolfe, 2001).
- Special-needs first graders acquired letter-sound and letter-recognition skills more easily when pictures mnemonics were integrated (Fulk, Lohman, & Belfiore, 1997).
- Mnemonics help activate the creation of stronger neuro-links in the hippocampus, which are essential to short- and long-term memory (Jensen, 2001).
- The ancient Greeks considered the imagination and high-level thinking needed for the creation of mnemonics as essential to a classical education (Wolfe, 2001).
- The use of mnemonic strategies have helped students with disabilities significantly improve their academic achievement (Forness, Kavale, Blum, & Lloyd, 1997).
- Two recent studies on using mnemonics for social studies instruction showed not only test improvement among all students but also marked improvement among students

with disabilities (Mastropieri, Sweda, & Scruggs, 2000; Uberti, Scruggs, & Mastropieri, 2003).

- Mnemonic instruction facilitates access to the general education curriculum by giving students the tools they need to better encode information so that it will be much easier to retrieve it from memory at later points (Access Center, 2007).
- Because facts are particularly difficult for the human brain to store and recall, mnemonics provide an avenue to verbal learning (Clark, 1999).
- Students who have been taught strategies for creating their own mnemonics outperform comparison students in free-study conditions (Mastropieri & Scruggs, 1998).
- Mnemonic instruction has been recommended as a practice with solid research evidence of effectiveness for individuals with learning disabilities (Access Center, 2006).

Thinking with Mnemonics in the Classroom

MODEL

Although there are a number of mnemonic devices, the authors have selected the following strategies that they believe best support the teaching of metacognition.

Mastropieri and Scruggs (1991) describe three steps involved in the use of the keyword mnemonic method:

- Reconstruct the term to be learned into an acoustically similar, already familiar, and easily pictured concrete term - select a keyword.
- Relate the keyword to the to-be-learned information in an interactive picture, image, or sentence.
- Retrieve the appropriate response by thinking of the keyword, the picture, and what was happening in the picture. State the information.

Modeling Mastropieri and Scruggs (1991) keyword method (Figure 5.1) could look something like this:

"Sometimes when I'm trying to remember new words and their meanings, it helps me to create some mental pictures or stories to help me remember. I'm going to show you what I mean with the word "superficial". One of the definitions that Webster gives for superficial is, *"of or being on the surface"*. The image that I'm going to create is a fish in a soup can floating on the surface of a pond."

Figure 5.1 Keyword Method

"I picked this mnemonic device because the word sounds like 'soup' and 'fish' and it means 'on the surface.'" This approach will help me remember because when I see the word *superficial* I'm going to remember the image that I created of a fish in a soup can. It will help me to remember how to pronounce the word and also what the word means."

Another mnemonic device for creating keywords for new vocabulary is LINCS (Ellis, 1992). Modeling the LINCS strategy to learn the vocabulary word "catapult" would take place such as this: (The teacher would be using the whiteboard or an interactive board to create visuals to accompany the modeling.)

"I'm going to show you something to use to help you remember vocabulary words. This strategy is the LINCS strategy and it will help you link new words to things that you already know. I'm going to show you what each letter of the

LINCS strategy stands for and how you can use them to help you remember new words. First, the" L" stands for list, so you need to List the parts. Write the word on a study card, and list the most important parts of the definition on the back. I know that I need to write the word "catapult" the front side of the card because it is the word to be defined. On the backside of the card I'm going to write "to throw or launch as if by an ancient device for hurling missiles." That is the definition of the word. I'm also going to think about that definition and make sure that I know what *hurling missiles* means."

"Now I'm going to explain the **"I"**, which stands for *imagine the picture.* I need to create a mental picture and describe it. For example, in my mind I need to see something being launched or thrown somehow over or through a barrier."

"I'm going to explain the **"N"** which stands for *note a reminding word.* So I'm thinking of a familiar word or words that sound like the vocabulary word. For example, a "cat" and a "pole" because "pole" sounds similar to "pult". I'm going to write these words on the bottom half of the card under the actual word to be learned."

"Next, let's talk about the **"C"** which stands for *Construct a LINCing (linking) story.* I'm going to make up a short story about the meaning of the word that includes the word to be remembered, for example, a cat pole-vaulting over a castle wall. I picked castle wall because the definition said an "ancient device" and I know that often castles are shown in ancient times."

"The **"S"** stands for *Self-Test.* This is where we are going to test our memory forward to back. Let's look at the word "catapult" and "cat pole" on the front of the card, and say aloud the definition on the back of the card, as well as, think about the image of a cat pole-vaulting over a castle wall. Next, let's reverse this process by looking at the back of the card to self-test the vocabulary word and keyword" (Foil & Alber, 2002).

The mnemonic "IT FITS" (King-Sears, Mercer, & Sindelar, 1992) is an acronym providing the following steps to create mnemonics for vocabulary words: Teacher modeling of this strategy could play out similar to the following example.

"I'm going to show you another strategy for helping to remember vocabulary words. It's called, "IT FITS". Each letter of "IT FITS" stands for something that we need to do to help us remember. I'm picking a hard vocabulary word because I want you to see how well this strategy will work." The word that I'm going to use is "impecunious".

"The first thing that I need to do is to *identify the term* or vocabulary word and we're using the word, "impecunious". That is the **"I"** of IT FITS. Next, I need to *tell the definition of the term*, which is "having no money". This step is the **"T"**. We now have the **"I"** and the **"T"** of "IT FITS." Then, we need to *find a keyword* that goes along with the definition and I'm going to say, "penniless imp". This gives us the **"Fi"** of our acronym. And now I need to *think about the definition* as it relates to the keyword, and imagine the definition doing something with the keyword. For example, "an imp tried to buy something but found that his pockets contained no money." This step provided the **"T"**. Finally, I need to *study what I imagined* until I know the definition" (Foil & Alber, 2002). The last step is the **"S"** step."

"I want to recap those steps for you. The letters of the acronym "IT FITS" stand for:

- **Identify** the term or word
- **Tell** the definition
- **Find** a keyword
- **Think** about the definition as it relates to the keyword
- **Study** what was imagined until the word is known

"When I need to remember a new vocabulary word the IT FITS acronym is a memory aid that I'll remember to use."

Teachers instruct students in the use of mnemonic strategies by using both visual and verbal cues. Keyword mnemonics can either be provided by the teacher or created by the student. However, it may be more effective for the teacher to provide the keyword mnemonics to the students (King-Sears et al., 1992; Scruggs & Mastropieri, 1992).

Teachers will have several opportunities to incorporate and model mnemonics in instruction. The important thing to remember is to explain to the students why the mnemonic device is being used and why it will work. For example, don't just tell students to remember the word "HOMES" to recall the Great Lakes. Explain to them that each letter represents the first letter of the name of each of the five Great Lake, Huron, Ontario, Michigan, Erie, and Superior. They need to understand that the letters act as triggers for their memories. Some additional examples of mnemonics are:

Acronyms

- "RAVEN" to help students remember when to use the word "affect" or "effect". Remember affect (is a) verb, effect (is a) noun.
- "McHale" is an acronym to assist with recalling forms of energy: mechanical, chemical, heat, atomic, light and electrical.

Rhymes or Phrases

- There are two **a**'s in calendar: one for **A**pril, the other for **A**ugust.
- Thirty days have September, April, June, and November. All the rest have thirty-one, except February, which has twenty-eight and in leap year twenty-nine.
- Dessert has two "**s**'**s**" because it involved something sweet; desert has one "**s**" because it involves **s**and.
- **E**migrants **e**xit, **I**mmigrants come **in**.
- The princi**pal** is your **pal**.

Chaining

When modeling chaining, the teacher would share something like this. "To help me remember things in a certain order, I sometimes make up silly stories, I find that the sillier the story that I can put in my mind, the easier I remember. Here's the silly story that I made up for the steps in long division. Farmer John has to *divide* up the food everyday for his *multiplying* bunnies. He *subtracts* what they ate and writes it in his journal. He *compares* how much they ate everyday and when the food bucket is empty, he climbs up into the loft to get more food to *bring down* for the bunnies. He keeps doing this everyday until there is no more food left in the loft for him to bring down."

In this example, the teacher is chaining the sequential steps to solving a long division problem; divide, multiply, subtract, compare, and bring down. The story also includes that you keep going until there is nothing left to bring down. Chaining is useful when students need to remember words or ideas that seem unrelated. The silly story helps students to attach meaning and thus, retain the required information.

It is important to note that the examples are only presented to aid in sparking creativity. Teachers have developed mnemonics since teaching began.

The ancient Greeks included the study of mnemonics (Wolfe, 2001). The "fun" part of this strategy is that the teacher can be as creative or silly as he or she desires. The more novel the image or idea, the more potential exists for student retention. When one of the authors was teaching fourth grade, one mnemonic used was this original story to help her students remember how to spell the word "tomorrow". The story goes like this. "John and Mary were planning a romantic boat ride for the next day. John told Mary that Tom was going to come with them. Mary said that she wanted to go with just John. John told Mary that Tom had the boat motor, so, "It's Tom or row." The story helps students remember that the word has two R's and not two M's. A silly little story will stick with students for years to come, so teachers can't be intimidated about creating such stories for their students.

Engage

It has been indicated in research that the success realized by young students with memory tasks relates to their age and academic maturity. They experience difficulty with memory related tasks. Learning-disabled students encounter similar difficulty with memory-related tasks and as a result, present greater potential for learning difficulties. They don't often create their own memory-triggering strategies or automatically know when a specific strategy is appropriate to use for a specific task. On the other hand, higher-achieving students are more apt to create their own strategies and also employ the strategies of others in an appropriate way. The good news is that all groups of students can be taught the types of memory aids described in this chapter and also when to use the mnemonics (Wolfe, 2001).

One strategy that is essential in memory is rehearsal. Rehearsal is appropriate to include in the engagement section of the text because rehearsal truly engages the learner. Rehearsal is not simply referring to repetition of facts, or rote rehearsal; but rather more elaborate rehearsal leading toward improved and increased comprehension of content. Wolfe (2001) states that "elaborative rehearsal" can bring about increased understanding and retention of information. Because elaborative rehearsal helps the learner to make meaning of the information, the opportunity for retention is increased. The mnemonic creates the hook on which the new learning can be attached.

One way to bring about engagement with rehearsal is with peer teaching. With their study partners, one student acts as the teacher and the other takes on the role of the learner. The teacher-student actually teaches the information just presented to his or her study partner. At a later point in the lesson, the roles are reversed. The 10:2 Theory (Rowe, 1986) is effective in bringing about engagement in this instance. The teacher teaches for ten minutes and then the peer teaching strategy can provide the two-minute processing time.

Let's now consider the strategies discussed in the Model segment of this chapter. To initiate the engagement piece of instruction, ask students to think aloud with their study partner and reflect about the process they used to learn the new vocabulary or content. The Think Pair Share activity described in the chapter on "Thinking Aloud" lends itself nicely to engagement at this point of strategy instruction. Engagement will vary depending on the mnemonic device that the teacher is implementing. Teachers may choose to engage students orally, or have them use the written strategies modeled in the previous section. The LINCS strategy provides the students with the opportunity to actually complete vocabulary note cards and include each of the steps framed by the acronym. The IT FITS strategy lends itself to oral practice and engagement with a study partner. As an additional form of engagement, teachers have the option to have students complete the thinking map, Figure 5. 2, and also explain orally the chosen process.

The strategy I used to help me remember is

This strategy helped me because

Other places that I will use this strategy are

Figure 5.2 Engagement Thinking Map

Transfer

In order for the mnemonic device to be effective and beneficial to students, transfer needs to occur. We need to know that the students will be able to use the strategy in various situations and call upon it independently. This will not occur quickly. A great deal of practice needs to be provided with the teacher scaffolding the process for the students.

One way to support transfer is to actually provide students with the opportunity to use the strategies that were presented earlier in the chapter in various learning situations. In one of the previous examples, the authors discussed the keyword strategy and provided the illustration of fish in the soup can to trigger understanding of the term *superficial*. In this case, transfer can occur by asking students to select a term from math, science, social studies or a piece of literature that they're reading, and instruct them to develop their own image for the term. This will help students to see that the keyword strategy will not only support their understanding of terms in the discipline where the strategy was taught, but that it can be useful in all subject areas. Ask them to work with an adult in their home to develop an image for a term that would help them in their real-life environment as well. Providing students with a *keyword* notebook that can be used to record their images and terms will encourage the transfer of the strategy.

Playing a game such as, "Where Can I Use It?" also promotes transfer. After teaching the chosen mnemonic strategy, ask students to list as many places that they can think of where they would use the strategy. Students listing the most appropriate places win the game. The lists should be shared with the group because the sharing will spark ideas in other students and will serve as a catalyst for their own further transfer.

Many of the graphic organizers presented in the appendix lend themselves to the transfer component of instruction. Encourage students to consider other areas of their academic lives and out-of-school lives where the strategies could be useful. Be prepared to talk them through the transfer aspect for several practice sessions, particularly when working with less mature learners.

It is also recommended to select one or two strategies and make sure that the students understand the strategy and how to use it before introducing additional new strategies. The goal is to provide strategies to support and promote learning. By introducing too many strategies too soon, frustration can result and the benefits of mnemonics may be lost.

Assess

Assessment should be considered formative when thinking about mnemonics. Peer teaching is an excellent opportunity for formative assessment through teacher monitoring. By monitoring the "teaching" of the teacher-student, the classroom teacher is able to determine whether or not the learning took place. Misconceptions and misunderstandings can be addressed on the spot. Wolfe (2001) suggests a variation of peer teaching that she refers to as "Double Check". This strategy would be appropriate for more mature learners in any content area. Students are instructed to work with their partner to read a segment in the text. Next, with the book closed, one student paraphrases what was read. The other partner checks the speaker for accuracy. An additional step would be to instruct the speaker to also share any mnemonic devices employed during the activity.

Checking students' notebooks can provide the teacher with feedback as to whether or not the mnemonics are being used by their students. By making the students aware that you will be looking for the use of mnemonics, it will increase the likelihood of the students consciously including them in their note-taking and studying.

Refer to the appendix with graphic organizers as a springboard for mnemonic assessment as well. After students have had the chance to independently work with the graphic organizer, the teacher should review it to determine whether or not the strategy has been learned.

Classroom Snapshot: On Your Own

Reflect on what you now know regarding mnemonic devices and record how this will look in your classroom.

1. What is a mnemonic device?
2. Why should I use a mnemonic device?
3. How would I use a mnemonic device?
4. How can I integrate mnemonic devices into my lessons to engage students' metacognitive skills?

Investigating Further

PRINT

Mastropieri, M. A., & Scruggs, T. E. (1991). *Teaching students ways to remember: Strategies for learning mnemonically.* Cambridge, MA: Brookline Press.

> An outstanding book that focuses on using mnemonic techniques to help students acquire basic skills, concepts, facts, and systems of facts—what mnemonic instruction facilitates most. Section 1 explains the major mnemonic techniques and the applications for which each is best suited. Section 2 demonstrates applications in specific subject areas—social studies, science, mathematics, and reading—indicating the suitable mnemonic techniques for tasks within each area, with a sample lesson applying each strategy. Many examples are presented.

Uberti, H. Z., Scruggs, T. E., & Mastropieri, M. A. (2003). Keywords make the difference! Mnemonic instruction in inclusive classrooms. *Teaching Exceptional Children*, 10(3), 56–61.

> This article describes a study where students in three inclusive third-grade classes were taught story vocabulary using the keyword method, vocabulary words with pictures, or vocabulary with definitions. The keyword method was more effective in increasing vocabulary learning. Using the keyword method, the achievement of students with learning disabilities matched students without disabilities.

Willoughby, T., & Wood, E. (1995). Mnemonic strategies. In E. Wood, V. E. Woloshyn, & T. Willoughby (Eds.), *Cognitive strategy instruction for middle and high schools* (pp. 5-17). Cambridge, MA: Brookline Press.

> The chapter on mnemonic strategies in this text provides a detailed discussion of mnemonic instructional materials and procedures.

WEB RESOURCES

MNEMONIC INSTRUCTION
http://www.teachingld.org/ld_resources/alerts/5.htm
> Provides general information and resources on mnemonics with an emphasis on working with students with learning disabilities.

THE VIRGINIA COUNCIL FOR LEARNING DISABILITIES
http://www.vcld.org/
> Provides information from Mastropieri and Scruggs. This reference provides information regarding each of the three methods mentioned in this document, as well as information regarding general techniques, training for independent use, and limitations.

THE CENTER FOR RESEARCH ON LEARNING AT THE UNIVERSITY OF KANSAS
http://www.ku-crl.org/
> Provides a quick one-page, on-line reference that demonstrates word-based devices and combined mnemonic devices. Illustrations provide examples for clearer understanding.

DIVISION FOR LEARNING DISABILITIES
http://www.dldcec.org/about/activities.html
> Members of the Division for Learning Disabilities (DLD) of the Council for Exceptional Children can access a free on-line tutorial on mnemonics.

THE NATIONAL CENTER ON ACCESSING CURRICULUM
http://www.cast.org/publications/ncac/index.html
> Publishes two information briefs, Teaching Sounds, Letters, and Letter-Sound Correspondences and These Methods Suggest a New Pedagogy for Literacy Development, which demonstrate how mnemonics are used in the classroom.

MNEMONIC STRATEGIES AND TECHNIQUES
http://education.stateuniversity.com/pages/2241/Mnemonic-Strategies-Techniques.html#ixzz0XkHui9Ut
> Article documenting components of mnemonic techniques and varieties and uses of mnemonic techniques as well as numerous successful educational applications of mnemonic techniques.

REFERENCES

Access Center. (2006). *Using Mnemonic Instruction to Facilitate Access to the General Education Curriculum.* Retrieved November 09, 2009. Available: http://www.ldonline.org/article/15577.

Clark, D. (1999). *Learning Domains or Bloom's Taxonomy.* Retrieved November 25, 2009. Available: http://www.nwlink.com/~donclark/hrd/bloom.html

Ellis, E. (1992). LINCS: *A starter strategy for vocabulary learning.* Lawrence, KS: Edge.

Forness, S. R., Kavale, K. A., Blum, I. M., & Lloyd, J. W. (1997). Mega-analysis of meta analysis: What works in special education and related services. *Teaching Exceptional Children, 29*(6), 4–9.

Fulk, B. M., Lohman, D., & Belfiore, P. J. (1997). Effects of integrated picture mnemonics on the letter recognition and letter-sound acquisition of transitional first grade students with special needs. *Learning Disability Quarterly, 20*(1), 33-42.

Jensen, J. (2001). *Arts with the brain in mind.* Alexandria, VA: Association for Supervision and Curriculum Development.

King-Sears, M. E., Mercer, C. D., & Sindelar, P. T. (1992). Toward independence with keyword mnemonics: A strategy for science vocabulary instruction. *Remedial and Special Education, 13,* 22-33.

Levin, J. R. (1993). Mnemonic strategies and classroom learning: A twenty-year report card. *The Elementary School Journal, 94*(2), 235-244.

Levin, M. E., & Levin, J. R. (1990). Scientific mnemonomies: Methods for maximizing more than memory. *American Educational Research Journal, 27,* 301-321.

Markowitz, K., & Jensen, E. (1999). *The great memory book.* San Diego, CA: The Brain Store.

Mastropieri, M. A., & Scruggs, T. E. (1998). Enhancing school success with mnemonic strategies. *Intervention in School and Clinic, 33*(4), 201-208.

Mastropieri, M. A., Sweda, J., & Scruggs, T. E. (2000). Teacher use of mnemonic strategy instruction. *Learning Disabilities Research and Practice, 15,* 69–74.

Rowe, M. B. (1986). Wait time: Slowing down may be a way of speeding up. *Journal of Teacher Education, 37*(43). Retrieved February 11, 2010. Available: http://jte.sagepub.com/cgi/content/abstract/37/1/43

Uberti, H. Z., Scruggs, T. E., & Mastropieri, M. A. (2003). Keywords make the difference! Mnemonic instruction in inclusive classrooms. *Teaching Exceptional Children*, 10(3), 56–61.

Wolfe, P. (2001). *Brain matters: Translating research into classroom practice.* Alexandria, VA: Association for Supervision and Curriculum Development.

CHAPTER SIX

Thinking Maps

Kolencik/Hillwig

"A picture is worth a thousand words."

Chinese proverb

This chapter investigates thinking maps, also known as graphic organizers or concept maps. Presented as an effective metacognitive strategy used to visually organize ideas, thinking maps illustrate relationships to launch and guide classroom discussion and serve as a visual representation of the thought processes used when studying content.

What Are the Nuts and Bolts?

Thinking maps, also known as graphic organizers, mind or concept maps, knowledge maps, story maps, cognitive organizers, or advance organizers, are instructional tools used to visually represent and depict the relationships between facts, terms, and/or ideas within a learning task. According to Black and Black (1990), "Thinking maps are mental maps that represent key skills like sequencing, comparing and contrasting, and classifying, and involve students in active thinking" (p. 2). These mental maps depict complex relationships and promote clearer understanding of content lessons. Thinking maps "become a metacognitive tool to transfer the thinking processes to other lessons which feature the same relationships" (Black & Black, 1990, p. 2).

Jones, Palincscar, Ogle, and Carr (1987) say that "graphic organizers and graphic outlines systems with frames and procedures for summarizing can be powerful tools to help students locate, select, sequence, integrate, and restructure information—both from the perspective of understanding and from the perspective of producing information in written responses" (p. 38).

According to McTighe and Lyman (1992), thinking maps serve as effective instructional tools for assisting both teachers and students in the following ways:

- Represent abstract or implicit information in a more concrete form,
- Depict relationships between facts and concepts,
- Generate and organize ideas for writing,
- Relate new information to prior knowledge,
- Store and retrieve information, and assess student thinking and learning (p. 81).

In *Classroom Instruction that Works: Research Based Strategies for Increasing Student Achievement*, by Robert J. Marzano, Debra Pickering, and Jane E. Pollack (2001), it is suggested that all graphic organizers can be placed into six common patterns:

- Descriptive Patterns
- Time-Sequence Patterns
- Process/Cause-Effect Patterns
- Episode Patterns
- Generalization/Principle Patterns
- Concept Patterns

Marzano feels that graphic organizers are the "most common way to help students generate nonlinguistic representation" (Marzano et al., 2001, p. 75). Marzano also cites *Educational Technology Research and Development* by Gerlic and Jausovec (1999), where the authors write that "engaging students in the creation of nonlinguistic representations stimulates and increases activity in the brain" (p. 73).

Merkley and Jefferies (2001) offer specific suggestions for teaching with graphic organizers. Their guidelines include verbalizing relationships between the concepts represented within the organizer, providing opportunities for student input, connecting new information to past learning, making reference to upcoming text, and reinforcing decoding and structural analysis. Thinking maps provide the opportunity to focus attention on key elements and distinguish among big ideas, little ideas, and supporting details. Table 6.1 includes examples of various types of thinking maps.

Thinking Map Type	Purpose
Descriptive Map Thematic Map	Effective for mapping generic information, but particularly well for mapping hierarchical relationships
K-W-L Chart	Effective for organizing information before, during, and after the learning
Network Tree Classification Chart	Organizing a hierarchical set of information, reflecting superordinate or subordinate elements
Spider Map	Use when the information relating to a main idea or theme does not fit into a hierarchy
Problem and Solution Map	Useful for organizing information when provided cause and effect problems and solutions
Problem-Solution Outline	Helps students to compare different solutions to a problem
Sequential Episodic Map Cause-Effect Chart	Useful for mapping cause and effect
Fishbone Map	Useful when cause-effect relationships are complex and non-redundant
Comparative and Contrastive Map Compare-Contrast Matrix Concept Web Venn Diagram	Helps students to compare and contrast two concepts according to their features; Compare concepts' attributes
Continuum Scale	Effective for organizing information along a dimension such as less to more, low to high, and few to many
Series of Events Chain Sequence/Flow Chart	Helps students organize information according to various steps or stages.
Cycle Map	Useful for organizing information that is circular or cyclical, with no absolute beginning or ending
Human Interaction Outline	Effective for organizing events in terms of a chain of action and reaction (especially useful in social sciences and humanities)

Table 6.1 Types of Thinking Maps

According to Hall and Strangman (2002), graphic organizers come in many different forms, each one best suited to organizing a particular type of information to address the teaching of metacognitive skills. The previous examples are merely a sampling of the different types and uses of thinking maps. An excellent way to integrate technology into the classroom, related to thinking maps, is to use Inspiration or Kidspiration software. Although the software is not free, it is very beneficial for the development of writing and higher order thinking.

What Does the Research Say?

Both theory and research strongly support the use of thinking maps as an active learning strategy.

- The mind arranges and stores information in an orderly fashion (Ausubel, 1968).
- Creating graphic organizers to illustrate the organization of ideas and information aids comprehension and learning (Flood & Lapp, 1988).
- Graphic organizers have been applied across a range of curriculum subject areas. Although reading is by far the most well studied application, science, social studies, language arts, and math are additional content areas that are represented in the research base on graphic organizers. (Hall & Strangman, 2005)
- Graphic organizers improving comprehension and more significantly improving vocabulary knowledge (Hall & Strangman, 2005).
- Graphic organizers can successfully improve learning when there is a substantive instructional context such as explicit instruction incorporating teacher modeling (Boyle & Weishaar, 1997; Gardill & Jitendra, 1999; Idol & Croll, 1987; Willerman & MacHarg, 1991).
- Operations such as mapping cause and effect, note taking, comparing and contrasting concepts, organizing problems and solutions, and relating information to main ideas or themes can be beneficial to many subject areas (Hall & Strangman, 2002).

- Graphic organizers embedded in a cooperative environment are more powerful teaching tools than teacher talk or conventional skill drill techniques. The graphic organizers are also tools for more sophisticated and authentic assessment approaches (Bellanca, 1992).
- Mind mapping engages all the brain's functions and captures the total picture (Buzan & Buzan, 1994).
- After examining 135 studies, Luiten concluded that forms of advanced organizers gave learners ways to conceptualize ideas, structure their thinking, better comprehend what they know and solidify the learning as theirs (Jensen, 1996).
- Graphic organizers meet the needs of students with a variety of learning styles and ability levels since they contain both visual and verbal information (Bromley, Irwin-DeVitis, & Modlo, 1995).
- Graphic organizers provide connections among bits of information, make information easier to remember, and allow students to break information into meaningful chunks (Parry & Gregory, 1998).
- Concepts mapping integrates the visual and the verbal which enhances understanding for concepts whether they are verbal, or nonverbal, concrete or abstract (Sousa, 1995).

Thinking Maps in the Classroom

MODEL

The authors write in the introductory portion of this work that, "Webster's dictionary states that the prefix meta- represents **after, beyond,** or **higher**. The authors contend that the strategies presented in this book challenge the reader to do just that; think beyond one's current thinking, reflect on one's thinking and move toward higher level thinking. Teachers should reflect after teaching and students' thinking will be improved after integrating the strategies. Students are being stretched beyond their current frame of thinking and moving toward the completion of much higher level tasks. The prefix sums up "the heartbeat of the book." Marzano, Pickering, and Pollock (2001) consider thinking maps or graphic organizers to be "nonlinguistic representations" and state that they should elaborate on knowledge. Following the line of thinking of Marzano and his colleagues, elaboration such as that with thinking maps is an excellent example of metacognition. Elaboration inclines us to think of something being completed with more detail. Metacognitive thinking is thinking with much more purposeful detail. It stands to reason that strategies involving thinking maps, graphic organizers, or whatever nomenclature chosen, should indeed be included in the strategies offered in this text.

Orlich et al. (2007) discuss graphic organizers as a means to, "illustrate learning hierarchies, principles of sequencing" (p. 156) and further states that graphic organizers "expedite and focus student learning" (p. 157). Examples of some graphic organizers included:

- Historical time lines
- Flow charts
- Graphs
- Tables
- Venn diagrams
- Content outlines

A very common organizer is the K-W-L chart. Many teachers have been incorporating this strategy perhaps without realizing that it is a metacognitive device. The students are encouraged to think about what they already know, what they want to learn and finally what they did learn. This self-reflection is an excellent tool to promote metacognition and is discussed in the earlier chapters of this text. Likewise, the Venn diagram is a common organizer and can be easily adapted to any grade level and any area of the curriculum. The Model and Engage section depicts how the use a Venn diagram might be incorporated into an effective instructional activity.

MODEL AND ENGAGE

For this particular example, model and engage are shown together since the students are actively engaged throughout the teaching segment.

When modeling a Venn diagram, one must keep in mind that it promotes higher level thinking. Through modeling the use of the graphic organizer, the teacher must use language that supports such higher level thinking. An instructional segment might be something like the following:

"Today we are going to compare and contrast the north and the south regions of the United States prior to the Civil War. You each have a blank column Venn diagram and we are going to use it to document our thinking about the two regions. On the Venn diagram, you have three columns. Label the left column North and the right column South." At this point the teacher would be modeling the labeling of the diagram on a white board, chalkboard, or perhaps with a computer program. "Under the section labeled North, we will note characteristics specific to the North and under South we will note characteristics for the South. The middle column will be used to note characteristics shared by both regions."

"With your partner, take the next sixty seconds to discuss one characteristic that would be specific to the North and jot it down under the appropriate section of the diagram". After the specified time, the teacher should ask the students to share some of their responses and write them on the teacher's column Venn diagram under the section labeled North. The same procedure would then be used for the section of the Venn labeled South. This type of instruction leads to thinking aloud and collaboration between students as well as instruction on the use of the Venn diagram.

After discussion and notation on the Venn diagram has been completed for the characteristics of the both regions, the instruction should move to the middle column of the Venn diagram. "Now that we have completed the diagram showing what we believe are the different characteristics of the North and the South, we need to consider characteristics that we believe to be shared by both. With your partner take the next sixty seconds to come up with two things that you believe would be the same in both regions." Following the same procedure described for the completion of the left and right columns of the Venn diagram, the middle section should be completed. Table 6.2, North and South Characteristics, is an example of a completed diagram.

North	Shared Characteristics	South
• Highly industrial • Large urban centers • Workers were free and paid for their labor	• Families were worried about war • Lincoln was president for both • Both thought that they were right	• More agricultural • Large plantations • Slaves worked fields • Wanted to be their own nation apart from the union of the United States

Table 6.2 North and South Characteristics

It should be explained that a Venn diagram is usually thought to be made up of overlapping circles, but the column Venn can be used for the same purpose and is often easier to design.

Transfer

Table 6.1 presented at the beginning of this chapter illustrates several examples of various types and purposes of thinking maps, thus, transfer to other curriculum areas or students' life outside of the school setting is facilitated. Since there is a thinking map to meet the "thinking" need for most situations, transfer with this strategy is anticipated. Once students have been exposed to the various types of thinking maps available and they recognize how thinking maps assist in organizing their thoughts, they will be more apt to utilize them. It is critical that the students be introduced to the use and value of the thinking maps at an early age. Thinking maps are easily adapted for use with all grade levels. Kindergarten students could use a Venn diagram and use illustrations in place of words in order to organize their thinking. The authors believe that transfer with the thinking maps strategy may be realized more naturally than with some of the other metacognitive strategies. Thinking maps are almost universal in that they can be used in conjunction with other metacognitive strategies. Throughout this text, teachers are encouraged to guide their students toward the use of thinking maps.

Assess

Assessment in the thinking map realm should be considered in two areas. First, the teacher must do some self-assessment when conducting instruction using the thinking map strategy. Teacher reflection should include the following self-questioning:

1. Was the thinking map strategy structured with purposeful talk leading to the outcome I desired for my students?
2. Did the thinking map instruction cover necessary thinking with this scenario?
3. Did I leave out any important thought processes that the students need to know?
4. Did I assume that they would know things and not verbalize them?

These are critical questions for self-assessment of instruction using the thinking map strategy.

Next, the assessment of the students' use of thinking maps could be formative; however, the teacher can use a thinking map as a summative assessment tool as well. Teacher observation and keeping running records could be one effective means of assessing the students' development of the thinking map strategy, but it can be easily adapted as a means of summative assessment. Considering the example given in the Model segment of this text, one could use a blank Venn diagram and instruct the students to list pre-Civil War characteristics of the North and the South as an alternative form of summative assessment. This assessment strategy would be an example of constructed response, differing greatly from the more traditional multiple choice or matching type of assessments.

Classroom Snapshot: On Your Own

Reflect on what you now know regarding the use of thinking maps and record how this will look in your classroom.

1. What is a thinking map?
2. Why should I use a thinking map?
3. How would I use a thinking map?
4. How can I integrate thinking maps into my lessons to engage students' metacognitive skills?

Investigating Further

PRINT

Barnekow, D. (2009). *3-D Graphic Organizers: 20 Innovative, Easy-to-Make Learning Tools That Reinforce Key Concepts and Motivate All Students.* New York: Scholastic.

Twenty engaging 3-D organizers with a ready-to-go templates, step-by-step directions, and ideas for using it across the curriculum. For use with Grades 3–6.

Bellanca, J. A. (2007). *A Guide to Graphic Organizers: Helping Students Organize and Process Content for Deeper Learning.* Thousand Oaks, CA: Corwin Press.

Offers teachers of all grade levels and content areas ready-to-use graphic organizers with guidelines for supporting cooperative learning groups, strengthening students' thinking processes, and developing effective assessments.

Bromley, K., Irwin-DeVitis, M., & Modlo, M. (1995). *Graphic Organizers.* New York: Scholastic Professional Books.

Practical handbook demonstrating how to use graphic organizers across the curriculum (K-8), as well as for planning, instruction, and assessment. Includes webs, Venn diagrams, cause-and-effect maps, cyclical organizers, and more. Provides ideas for developing graphic organizers to fit students' needs.

Drapeau, P. (2008). *Differentiating with Graphic Organizers: Tools to Foster Critical and Creative Thinking.* Thousand Oaks, CA: Corwin Press.

Demonstrates how to use, create, and modify graphics organizers to promote critical and creative thinking processes to raise achievement for students of all ability levels.

WEB RESOURCES

THE GRAPHIC ORGANIZER
http://www.graphic.org/index.html

> This site is a rich resource for learning about graphic organizers, offering links, lists of references and books about graphic organizers, information about using graphic organizers for writing, guidelines for designing graphic organizers and assisting students in designing them, and samples of student work with graphic organizers.

TOOLS FOR READING, WRITING, & THINKING
http://www.greece.k12.ny.us/instruction/ela/6-12/Tools/Index.htm

> This is a fantastic resource for graphic organizers. The graphic organizers are broken down by subject (reading or writing) and have a description of each document. You can also be directly linked to organizers that complement reading strategies, as well as rubrics for various writing and speaking activities.

FREE GRAPHIC ORGANIZERS
http://freeology.com/graphicorgs/page3.php

> Hundreds of templates for graphic organizers. All files are in PDF format and open in a separate window.

ONLINE TEACHER RESOURCE
http://www.teach-nology.com/web_tools/graphic_org/concept_web/

> Enables teachers to generate a wide variety of graphic organizers, puzzles, and rubrics.

REFERENCES

Ausubel, D. P. (1968). *Educational psychology: A cognitive view.* New York: Holt.

Bellanca, J. A. (1992). *The cooperative think thank II: Graphic organizers to teach thinking in the cooperative classroom.* Palatine, IL: Skylight Publishing, p. vi.

Black, H. & Black, S. (1990). *Organizing thinking: Graphic organizers, Book II.* Pacific Grove, CA: Midwest Publications Critical Thinking Press and Software.

Bromley, K., Irwin-DeVitis, L., & Modlo, M. (1995). *Graphic organizers: Visual strategies for active learning.* New York: Scholastic Professional.

Boyle, J. R., & Weishaar, M. (1997). The effects of expert-generated versus student-generated cognitive organizers on the reading comprehension of students with learning disabilities. *Learning Disabilities Research & Practice,* 12(4), 228-235.

Buzan, T., & Buzan, B. (1994). *The mind map book.* New York: NAL-Dutton.

Flood, J., & Lapp, D. (1988). "Conceptual mapping strategies for understand information texts." *The Reading Teacher,* 41(8), 780-783.

Gardill, M. C., & Jitendra, A. K. (1999). Advanced story map instruction: Effects on the reading comprehension of students with learning disabilities. *The Journal of Special Education,* 33(1), 2-17.

Gerlic, I., & Jausovec, N. (1999). Multimedia: Differences in cognitive processes observed with EEG. *Journal of Technology Research and Development,* 47(3), 5-14.

Hall, T., & Strangman, N. (2005). "Graphic Organizers." *National Center on Accessing the General Curriculum Publications.* Retrieved February 14, 2010 from Center for Applied Special Technology Universal Design for Learning http://www.cast.org/publications/ncac/ncac_go.html.

Hall, T., & Strangman, N. (2002). *Graphic organizers.* Wakefield, MA: National Center on Accessing the General Curriculum. Retrieved February 15, 2010 from http://www.cast.org/publications/ncac/ncac_go.html.

Idol, L., & Croll, V. J. (1987). Story-mapping training as a means of improving reading comprehension. *Learning Disability Quarterly,* 10(3), 214-229.

Jensen, E. (1996). *Completing the puzzle: The brain-based approach.* Del Mar, CA: Turning Point Publishing.

Jones, B. F., Palincsar, A. S., Ogle, D. S., & Carr, E. G. (Eds.). (1987). *Strategic teaching and learning: Cognitive instruction in the content areas.* Alexandria, VA: Association for Supervision and Curriculum Development.

Marzano, R., Pickering, D., & Pollack, J. E. (2002). *Classroom instruction that works: Research based strategies for increasing student achievement.* Alexandria, VA: ASCD, 2001.

McTighe, J., & Lyman, (1992). Mind tools for matters of the mind. In A. L. Costa, J. A. Bellanca, & R. Fogarty (Eds.), *If minds matter: A foreword to the future.* Volume II (pp.71-90). Palatine, IL: IRI/Skylight Publishing.

Merkley, D. M., Jeffries, D. (2001). Guidelines for implementing a graphic organizer. The Reading Teacher, 54(4), 350-357.

Orlich, D. C., Harder, R. J., Callahan, R. C., Trevisan, M. S., Brown, A. H. (2007). *Teaching strategies: A guide to effective instruction.* Boston, MA: Houghton Mifflin.

Parry, T., & Gregory, G. (1998). *Designing brain compatible learning.* Arlington Heights, IL: Skylight.

Sousa, D. (1995). *How the brain learns* (2nd ed.). Thousand Oaks, CA: Corwin Press.

Willerman, M., & MacHarg, R. A. (1991). The concept map as an advance organizer. *Journal of Research in Science Teaching,* 28(8), 705-712.

CHAPTER SEVEN

Thinking as a Reader

Kolencik/Hillwig

"Reading is merely a surrogate for thinking for yourself."

Arthur Schopenhauer (1788-1860)

"Read, every day, something no one else is reading.
Think, everyday, something no one else is thinking."

Christopher Morley (1890-1957)

Good readers also need to develop their metacognitive skills. This chapter examines explicit instructional strategies in order for students to become metacognitive readers.

What Are the Nuts and Bolts?

Metacognition is defined in the literacy world as comprehension monitoring, that is, being aware of one's level of understanding as one reads and then using this awareness to guide the reader. Good readers use metacognitive skills to self-monitor their reading. When students read, they self-regulate and try to make sense of the text. Metacognition enables readers to identify what they understand and what confuses them. Cognitive approaches to reading emphasize decoding and comprehending words, constructing meaning, and developing expert reader strategies. Metacognitively skilled readers seek to establish "meaningfulness" in their reading and value careful selection of appropriate strategies and careful monitoring of their comprehension (Palincsar & Brown, 1984).

Metacognition is involved in reading in the sense that good readers develop control of their own reading skills and understand how reading works. For example, good readers know that it is important to comprehend the meaning of what an author is saying. Teachers can help students develop good metacognitive strategies for reading by getting them to monitor their own reading, especially when they run into difficulties. Researchers (Pressley & Harris, 2006; Pressley & Hilden, 2006) suggest the following metacognitive strategies that teachers can help students use to improve their reading: 1) overview text before reading; 2) look for important information while reading and pay more attention to it than other information; ask yourself questions about the important ideas or relate them to something you already know; 3) attempt to determine the meaning of words not recognized (use the words around a word to figure out its meaning, use a dictionary, or temporally ignore it and wait for further clarification; 4) monitor text comprehension; 5) understand relationships between parts of the text; 6) recognize when you might need to go back and reread a passage you didn't understand or to clarify or remember an important idea, or to underline or summarize for study; and 7) adjust pace of reading depending on the difficulty of the material.

Mokhtari and Sheorey (2002) have designed a reading strategies inventory entitled, Metacognitive Awareness of Reading Strategies Inventory (MARSI). This student self-reporting instrument of 30 items, 13 global reading strategies, 8 problem solving strategies, and 9 support reading strategies can help classroom teachers discover what reading strategies their students use as it relies on students' metacognitive awareness and perceived use of their reading strategies. The MARSI can be extremely valuable to make teachers more aware of how students learn, thus, resulting in better instruction. The inventory is available online at http://www.docstoc.com/docs/21909421/Metacognitive-Awareness-of-Reading-Strategies-Inventory.

What Does the Research Say?

Findings from the published literature conclude that metacognition plays an important role in reading.

- The use of questions embedded in reading material encourages struggling readers...when students are controlled with questions during reading, they will more likely use proactive metacognitive strategies (Weir, 1998).
- Reading logs and self-assessment checklists promote metacognitive growth because these activities encourage students to reflect on their reading practices while monitoring their comprehension of a text (Swartzendruber-Putnam, 2000; Skeans, 2000).
- After reading a selection, engaging students in an ongoing discourse about thinking and learning promotes cognitive development (Paris & Paris, 2001).
- Teachers need an awareness of metacognitive research, recognizing that poor readers use self-reflective practices less often than good readers (Garner, 1994).
- The distinction between good and poor readers relates to the differences in metacognitive awareness (Kelleher, 1997).
- Teachers should know that poor readers make greater gains through metacognitive instruction than more skilled readers (Weir, 1998).
- Students' awareness of their own reading comprehension processes can be enhanced through systematic, direct instruction (Paris & Winograd, 1990).
- Metacognitive awareness is particularly important in proficient and skilled readers (Mokhtari & Sheorey, 2002).
- According to Onwugbuzie (2004) "reading comprehension represents the reader's ability to integrate effectively and meaningfully apply acquired knowledge with the information provided in the text" (p. 444).

The National Reading Panel (National Institute of Child Health and Human Development, 2000), in summarizing much of the aforementioned evidence, concluded that there are eight effective metacognitive strategies:

comprehension monitoring, cooperative learning, graphic and semantic organizers, story structure, question answering, question generation, summarization, and multiple-strategy use.

Model

There are many strategies to bear in mind when planning for modeling strategies to promote thinking readers. As a result, the authors' format of describing one or two teaching scenarios is being exchanged for a more comprehensive overview of several strategies to promote thinking as a reader.

When considering the modeling of strategies leading to proficiency as a thinking reader, it is critical to first discuss metacognitive skills and metacognitive strategies. Rachel Billmeyer (2001) states that there is a difference between the two and cites several examples. According to Billmeyer (2001), metacognitive skills include predicting, paraphrasing, and delaying decision making until different points of view are considered. Billmeyer (2001) further states, "Skills are mental activities that can be applied to specific learning situations. Having a skill is knowing how to perform a behavior" (p. 27). She elaborates by stating that strategies "are specific ways of executing a given skill, or knowing when to use the behavior" (p. 27). An example of a metacognitive strategy would be when the reader knows that comprehension of the text isn't occurring and realizing that re-reading the passage slower will support and promote understanding. The bottom line is simply that thinking as a reader requires that students have developed metacognitive skills, but that they also self-monitor and know when to apply a specific skill. Knowing when and how to use the skill evolves intro a metacognitive strategy. Research has indicated that students may have knowledge of metacognitive skills, but may not know when or how to apply them as strategies. A thinking reader is cognizant of when to use specific strategies and how to apply those strategies.

In Chapter 3, Thinking Aloud, the authors stressed the importance of teachers verbalizing their own thinking in a very explicit, step-by-step, manner. The teacher think aloud aligns naturally with modeling for the intended outcome of creating thinking readers. Students will increase the use of metacognitive strategies when the teachers model and think aloud their own self-regulating of thinking and understanding.

Through the teacher think aloud, questions such as, "I'm not quite sure what this passage means, what can I do to help myself understand?" "Should I slow down my reading pace and re-read this?" "Do I understand the meanings of individual words, or do I need to do some vocabulary work first?" "Do I have enough background knowledge about this topic to maximize my comprehension?" In this case, the teacher think aloud helps the student understand what goes on mentally to solve the problem of limited comprehension. Self-questioning is a critical component to becoming a thinking reader.

Teacher think alouds in conjunction with explicit instruction in summarizing, paraphrasing, and the use of thinking maps for use before, during and after reading support comprehension. A thinking reader actively constructs meaning during reading and it is beneficial to access prior knowledge before reading a passage in order to aid the construction of meaning. The well-known K-W-L chart previously discussed in this text is one example of a tool to assist learners call upon prior knowledge. A teacher-provided anticipation guide will also support comprehension and aid the students in developing background knowledge prior to engaging with the text. Strategic learners know that calling upon prior knowledge is key to being successful with new learning.

Thinking readers are aware of the importance of organizational patterns and organization of thinking. This organization can take place internally or externally, but strategic learners are proficient information organizers. There are several organizational patterns present in text including, but not limited to:, cause and effect, problem/solution, compare/contrast, and sequence of events. Many students will be able to organize the necessary information mentally, while others will benefit from a visual representation such as a thinking map. Venn diagrams, timelines, or concept webs are some examples of visual representations that would encourage organization of information.

Teacher modeling of the suggested examples is critical in the development of thinking readers. Self-questioning, calling upon prior knowledge and organizing information are just a few of the numerous strategies that can be employed to support the students' construction of meaning.

Engage

Billmeyer (2001) suggests three phases of thinking/learning: planning phase, during-learning phase, and reflecting phase. Student engagement is easily facilitated when the learning is framed in these three phases. The initial planning phase requires active engagement of the learners. The thinking reader is required to plan for the reading to take place and determine what and how to go about it. A plan for accessing prior knowledge, searching out problematic vocabulary, establishing a purpose for the reading, and determining the organizational structure of the text (narrative/informational) is necessary. Savage et al. (2006) state that one problem students face is not "recognizing the relevance" of background experiences. Teachers need to assist students in identifying the connection between prior knowledge and the present academic task. The use of advance organizers would be appropriate to support the students' recognition of the relevance of their prior knowledge. According to the Northeast Texas Consortium (2002), "an advance organizer helps to organize new material by outlining, arranging and sequencing the main idea of the new material based on what the learner already knows. Advance organizers use **familiar terms and concepts** to link what the students **already know** to the new information that will be presented in the lesson, which aids in the process of transforming knowledge and creatively applying it in new situations."

Savage et al. (2006) suggest ReQuest, a strategy designed by Manzo (1969). ReQuest is actually an acronym for "reciprocal questioning" and can be effective in the planning phase to help students relate prior knowledge. The teacher and the students read the first sentence or first few sentences together. The teacher then closes his or her book, but the students are able to refer back to the reading. The students then ask the teacher questions related to the passage just read. The teacher can make recommendations to improve the quality of the questions if deemed necessary. The students then close their books and the teacher poses questions that will help the students recall previous knowledge that would be relevant. This strategy not only provides a framework for accessing prior knowledge, but serves as a model for asking questions and directing students' reading. The student is actively engaged throughout this process.

The during-learning phase requires the thinking reader to organize information, self-monitor and self-question. Thinking maps assist the learner is organizing information being read, while questions such as, "Do I understand what I just read?", "What message is the author trying to convey to me?", "What do I need to do to be able to understand this passage better?", require the thinking reader to reflect on his or her own learning. This type of metacognitive monologue demonstrates that the learner is cognizant of his or her own thought processes. Educational researchers, such as Estes and Vaughan (1986) and Garner (1992), use two words; clunk and click, to describe readers' metacognitive process. When the answer is "no" to the question, "Do I understand this?", readers experience a clunk that informs them there is a need for strategic action. Understanding is described as the click of comprehension, telling readers that it's okay to continue (Estes & Vaughan, 1986; Garner, 1992). Study skills guides can be use during this phase of learning and could include questions such as, "What prediction can you make at this point?", "Can you paraphrase this section of the text?", "How would you summarize the passage in one sentence?" (Savage et al., 2006). At this point, the learner can determine whether or not the learning is on target and apply strategies to get back on track if necessary.

The reflective phase of the learning engages the learners through determining whether or not they accomplished the purpose for the reading, and integrated the new learning with prior knowledge. The thinking reader will be able to plan for ways to apply what was just learned to future situations. A skeletal note taking framework could be used to facilitate reflection, as well as journal entries. Should journal entries be used at this phase, the teacher should also include some leading questions to guide the learner toward self monitoring. Questions for consideration could include, "What did I do when I didn't understand what I read?" and "Why was I having difficulty understanding the passage?" It is critical to remember that the teacher is not only teaching the content, but the metacognitive strategies in an integrated manner. Self-reflection and self-assessment during this phase is metacognition in the truest form.

Transfer

Transfer occurs almost naturally for the thinking reader. The metacognitive strategies employed as a thinking reader aren't constrained to a specific content area, but rather easily and logically manifest themselves across the curriculum and outside of the school walls. Problem solving, self-monitoring, planning, and reflection are strategies that serve all individuals well in all areas of academic, personal, and professional life. Students at all grade levels must be proficient, thinking readers. The skills and strategies learned to become a thinking reader are valuable tools leading to lifelong, competent thinkers.

Assess

Assessment in the arena of Thinking as a Reader will be viewed in two tiers. Tier One will examine assessment of the reading process and Tier Two will focus on application of the metacognitive strategies.

When planning for Tier One assessment in reading, consider various assessment methods and cross-curricular data when possible. Traditional forms of assessment, as well as constructed-response, alternative assessments can be used to assess the reading process and ultimately reading comprehension. Billmeyer (2001) states that portfolios are beneficial in assessment because they provide various ways to collect data. She indicates that portfolios may include inventories about students' attitudes toward reading and the reading process, fluency checks, written responses to the reading and interviews. While portfolios may be effective, they present a huge time commitment on the teacher's part.

Tier Two assessment of the student in the realm of thinking as a reader, moves from the quantitative to the qualitative. Self-monitoring checklists and self-assessment forms are two examples of assessing the thinking reader. It is critical to keep in mind that the purpose of assessment is to determine what the learner knows and to identify and plan for improvement. The thinking reader must be encouraged to engage in a metacognitive monologue where self-questioning becomes automatic. An effective assessment of megacognitive literacy could take place in the form of journaling that includes questions such as:

- What strategies did I use in the planning phase of the reading/learning?
- What strategies did I use to activate my prior knowledge?
- What strategies did I use when I encountered a passage that was difficult to understand?
- What strategies did I use when I came upon vocabulary that was unfamiliar?
- What steps did I take to reflect upon the reading/learning?
- Did I use thinking maps or other visual organizers to organize my thinking?
- Did I use strategies that didn't work for me? Why didn't they work? Would they work in a different situation?

Teachers must be cognizant of the complexity of the reading process and understand that assessment must be multifaceted, with a clear purpose in mind. Assessments must be designed to actually elicit the type of information that is desired. Assessment of the strategies used by thinking readers is as critical as assessment of the actual process of reading and reading comprehension.

Classroom Snapshot: On Your Own

Reflect on what you have learned regarding thinking as a reader and record how this will look in your classroom.

1. What metacognitive reading strategies will I stress in my classroom?
2. Why should I use these metacognitive reading strategies?
3. How would I use these metacognitive reading strategies with my students?
4. How can I design reading lessons to engage students' metacognitive skills?

Investigating Further

PRINT

Hacker, D. J., Dunlosky, J., & Graesser, A. C. (1998). (Eds.), *Metacognition in educational theory and practice.* Mahwah, NJ: Lawrence Erlbaum.

>Fourteen chapters review many aspects of metacognition in education, including reading, writing, problem solving, and studying. Chapter 8 focuses on reading and the interaction between metacognitive strategies and cognitive strategies in reading.

Israel, S., Block, C. C., & Kinnucan-Welsch, K. (2005). *Metacognition in literacy learning: Theory, assessment, instruction, and professional development.* Mahwah, NJ: Lawrence Erlbaum.

>Useful summary of theory, research, and practice concerning the important role of metacognition in literacy learning; also offers insightful ideas and suggestions about metacognition and literacy.

Mokhtari, K., & Reichard, C. A. (2002). Assessing students' metacognitive awareness of reading strategies. Journal of Educational Psychology 94(2), 249-259.

>Describes the development and validation of the Metacognitive Awareness of Reading Strategies Inventory, which is designed to assess adolescent and adult readers' metacognitive awareness and perceived use of reading strategies while reading academic materials.

National Reading Panel. (2000). *Teaching children to read: An evidence-based assessment of the scientific research literature on reading and its implications for reading instruction.* (NIH Publication No. 00-4769). Washington, DC: U.S. Government Printing Office.

> This massive literature review of the peer-reviewed, published experimental research in K–12 reading summarizes 204 cognitive strategy instruction studies.

WEB RESOURCES

METACOGNITION AND READING
http://www.udel.edu/ETL/SARA/Bib_metacog.html

> Although a bit dated, this bibliography that was developed in the late 1990s contains references to more than 45 articles and other sources about metacognition and reading from childhood to adulthood.

METACOGNITIVE INTERVIEW FORM
http://www.ncrel.org/sdrs/areas/issues/students/learning/lr1metin.htm

> A sample metacognitive interview forms that ask students to explain how they went about reading a passage of text.

METACOGNITIVE READING COMPREHENSION STRATEGIES
http://www.readingrockets.org/article/3479

> Discusses seven researched-based strategies for improving text comprehension.

REFERENCES

Billmeyer, R. (2001). *Capturing all of the reader through the reading assessment system: Practical applications for guiding strategic readers.* Omaha, NE: Rachel & Associates, Inc.

Estes, T. H., & Vaughan, J. L. (1986). *Reading and reasoning beyond the primary grades.* Boston, MA: Allyn & Bacon.

Garner, R. (1992). "Metacognition and Self-Monitoring Strategies." In R. Ruddell (Ed.), Newark, DE: *What Research Has to Say about Reading Instruction* (2nd ed.).

Garner, R. (1994). "Metacognition and executive control." In R. Ruddell (Ed.), Newark, DE: *Theoretical models and processes of reading* (pp. 715-32). International Reading Association.

Kelleher, M. E.(1997). Readers' theatre and metacognition. *Reading Association Journal,* 33, 4-12.

Manzo, A. (1969). ReQuest: A method for improving reading comprehension through receiprocal questioning. *Journal of Reading,* 12, 123-126.

Mokhtari, K., & Sheorey, R. (2002). Measuring ESL students' awareness of reading strategies. *Journal of Developmental Education,* 25(3), 2–10.

National Institute of Child Health and Human Development. (2000). *Report of the National Reading Panel. Teaching children to read: An evidence-based assessment of the scientific research literature on reading and its implications for reading instruction.* (NIH Publication No. 00-4769) Washington DC: U.S. Government Printing Office.

Northeast Texas Consortium. (2002). Advance organizers: Creating and using advance organizers for distance learning. Retrieved August 30, 2010. Available at http://www.netnet.org/instructors/design/goalsobjectives/advance.htm.

Onwuegbuzie, A. J. (2004). Reading comprehension among African American graduate students. *Journal of Negro Education,* The. FindArticles.com. September 12, 2010. Available at http://findarticles.com/p/articles/mi_qa3626/is_200410/ai_n13506807/.

Palincsar, A., & Brown, A. (1984). Reciprocal teaching of comprehension-fostering and comprehension-monitoring activities. *Cognition and Instruction,* 1, 117-175.

Paris, S. G., & Paris, A. H. (2001). Classroom applications of research on self-regulated learning. *Educational Psychologist,* 36, 89-101.

Paris, S. G., & Winograd, P. (1990). How metacognition can promote academic learning and instruction. In B. F. Jones & L. Idol (Eds.), *Dimensions of thinking and cognitive instruction* (pp. 15-51). Hillsdale, NJ: Erlbaum.

Pressley, M., & Harris, K. (2006). Cognitive strategies instruction. In P. A. Alexander & P. H. Winne (Eds.), *Handbook of educational psychology* (2nd ed., pp. 265-286). Mahwah, NJ: Erlbaum.

Pressley, M., & Hilden, K. (2006). Cognitive strategies. In W. Damon & R. Lerner (Eds.), *Handbook of child psychology* (6th ed., pp. 512-547). New York: Wiley.

Savage, T.V., Savage, M.K., & Armstrong, D.G. (2006). *Teaching in the secondary school* (6th ed.). Upper Saddle River, NJ: Pearson Merrill Prentice Hall.

Skeans, S. (2000). "Reading... with Pen in Hand!" *English Journal*, 89, 69-72.

Swartzendruber-Putnam, D. (2000). Written reflection: Creating better thinkers, better writers. *English Journal*, 90, 88-93.

Weir, C. (1998). Using embedded questions to jump-start metacognition in middle school readers. *Journal of Adolescent & Adult Literacy*, 41(6), 458-467.

Metacognition in Action

CHAPTER EIGHT

Meta-Q: Thinking with Questioning

Kolencik/Hillwig

"The essence of education is not what we learn, but questioning what we learn."

Mark Taylor, teacher
Olathe South High School, 2010

The art of questioning is an effective practice worthy of development in the quest for enhanced metacognition. The authors use the term "art" of questioning because in some cases strategic questioning isn't innate, but needs to be developed, nurtured, and honed in order to be most valuable. Meta-Q questioning is questioning that moves the learner toward higher-level, complex thinking resulting in self-refection, self-monitoring, and self-regulating. Meta-Q considers both teacher-generated and student-generated questioning since both aspects play an important role in strengthening metacognition.

Let us begin by investigating the importance of improving questioning. Walsh and Sattes (2003) offer five reasons to support a focus on improving questioning. In their work, *QUILT: Questioning and Understanding to Improve Learning and Thinking*, they state that:

1. "Questioning is at the heart of learning", because in the cognitive domain questions initiate "the making of personal meaning" or "the making of connections" (Walsh & Sattes, 2003). They further discuss the affective domain of learning explaining that questions "stimulate curiosity and motivate the individual learner" (Walsh & Sattes, 2003).
2. "Questioning is at the heart of teaching" because of the many roles that questioning plays in the teaching process. Questions can be utilized to stress critical content, to check understanding, or to trigger prior knowledge in students.
3. In the age of information it is critical for learners to know "how and where to access information".
4. "Questioning stimulates thinking and is a tool for problem solving, decision making, and other important cognitive processes" (Walsh & Sattes, 2003, p. 23).
5. It has been indicated through research that many educators don't vary the approach to questioning in order to maximize student learning.

After several decades of research on questioning, it has been noted that teachers use a great deal of instructional time asking questions. Teachers tend to ask 20 to 60 questions in each typical class period (Walsh & Sattes, 2003). The concern isn't that teachers don't ask questions. The concern is that teachers don't vary the questions or question in a manner that promotes higher level and metacognitive thinking. Research has shown that in many cases teachers ask fact-based, lower level questions that don't move learners beyond basic recall. Hunkins (1995) states that questioning should be viewed as a means to aid students in generating concepts and relationships and not simply as a way to assess the "specifics of learning". With Hunkins' view in mind, we are considering questions that aren't specifically designed with one correct answer in mind as much as questions that lead to more questions or more complex student thinking.

Questioning has been shown to be effective before, during and after instruction, although the questioning format and design should be different for the various instructional segments (Wilen, 1987). Chapter 2 of this text discusses in detail questioning before, during, and after lessons and offers a more extensive list of examples. A few examples of these questions are noted here. Before introduction of new content, questions that activate prior knowledge are appropriate. Starters like: "Tell what you know about _____", or "Summarize what you have learned so far about_____", should be posed as a means to access prior learning. Meta-Q questions posed at the start of a lesson segment are an excellent example of metacognition due to the self-monitoring and self-reflection that they trigger.

During instruction, questions that elicit recitation or provide guided practice are effective and questioning during instruction also serves to keep students on-task and motivated with the learning at hand. Depending on the content and age level of the students, the types of questions may vary. Questioning during the lesson can actually direct the student toward more in depth, complex thinking. "What are you thinking about right now?", or "How has your thinking about this topic changed since we began this discussion?" are examples of Meta-Q questions during the lesson. Many of the questions posed in this phase of instruction won't have one correct answer, but actually can lead to the development of further questions and the creation of concepts and relationships (Hunkins, 1995).

Wilen (1987) states that after instruction, questioning can be in the form of review of content, seatwork, quizzes, or homework. Questioning after instruction is an effective way to review the learning prior to moving onto new content or closing the learning episode. Depending on the structure of the questions, they can guide the learner toward more complex thinking and development of desired relationships and concepts. Specific examples, listed in Chapter 2, that trigger more complex thinking are "Summarize what you have learned today about____", "Write a revised definition of _____", or "How will you use the information you learned today?"

Walsh and Sattes (2003) cite the work of Meredith Gall stating that questions help to motivate and focus students, aid in more profound information processing, provide the chance for practice and allow students to self-monitor and determine their understanding and mastery of the new learning. Since questions present such varied, positive, contributions to student learning, it is important to look thoroughly at what good teacher questioning should look like.

The questions that teachers develop and present have great impact on **what** students learn. Students attend to information that aligns with teacher questions and often, students consider that teacher-questions indicate content that the teacher considers to be important. If the teacher asks only basic recall, fact-based questions, the student may inadvertently overlook opportunities for more in-depth thought and learning through additional sources such as the text and independent study. Teachers must ensure that their questioning skills are developed and utilized in order to facilitate higher level thinking and metacognition in their students.

Teacher questioning affects **how much** students learn and also **which** students access the learning. Research has shown that students that are more actively engaged and ask and answer more questions experience increased learning and achievement. In other words, students that get called upon more often, learn more. Now let's look at the fact that research also tells us that teachers tend to call upon more academically successful students more often than less academically successful students. So what does this tell us? The more questions a student asks and answers results in greater academic achievement, but teachers tend to call upon the academically weaker student less often. It is a double-edged sword. Students need to be called upon to learn more, but the students that need it the most, tend to be called upon the least amount of times.

Another very simple issue dealing with calling upon students is related to classroom logistics. The area within the teacher's line of vision is often the area that gets the most teacher attention. As a result of this information, teachers need to make sure to equitably engage all students in questioning, providing opportunities for responding to all students.

In the arena of teacher questioning it should be stated that more questions aren't necessarily better. It is far better to pose a few well-developed, purposeful questions than 40 or 50 random, fact-based questions that don't move students beyond the basic cognitive level. Questions need to be prepared in advance and should spotlight the critical content of the lesson, be congruent with the lesson objective/s and be presented in a very clear manner.

The following self-assessment may assist teachers with development of Meta-Q questions:

o   Did I prepare a few purposeful questions in advance of the lesson?
o   Do the questions align with the lesson objective/s?
o   Are the questions only fact-based? If yes, how can I change the question/s to move toward Meta-Q questions that entail higher cognitive level thinking from my students?
o   Are the questions planned with clear, easily understood language?

Student-Generated Questions

When considering Meta-Q questions, one can't overlook the important role that student questions play in the learning process. Student questions not only support learning and making meaning of the new content, but also aid in self-regulating learning and reflection. Walsh and Sattes (2003) in QUILT offer the following rationales supporting student questions:

- "Questions are invitations to others to engage in conversation." Learning is considered a social activity, thus students need to be comfortable with their ability and the learning environment in order to ask questions of their teachers and/or peers. "Skilled questioners have communicative competence."

- It is as important to be aware of "not knowing" and to be able to then generate a question that will address what it is that isn't fully understood. Walsh and Sattes quote classroom questioning authority, J. T. Dillon, stating, "If they (students) are able to frame a question about a concept or fact, they already have at least two thirds of the answer."

- Questions can move the student toward a heightened level of curiosity where he or she desires understanding and is "unwilling to remain ignorant about the issue in question."

- Hunkins (1995) states, "Questions should be tools that students employ actively in their learning, not just some device." According to him, "Students need to be in the driver's seat regarding questioning."

Ciardiello (1998) discusses the importance of questions in the article "Did You Ask a Good Question Today?" Ciardiello tells of the mother of Isidore I. Rabi, Nobel laureate in physics. Rabi's mother didn't ask her son what he learned in school each day, but instead asked him if he asked a good question. Rabi indicated that asking good questions made the difference and led him to become a scientist. Ciardiello further states that "Research has indicated that an explicit system of training is a major requirement for successful student generation of higher level questions." In her memory-focused website, McPherson (2001) contends that students should be taught to generate and ask the following types of questions:

1. Comprehension questions (e.g., What is this problem all about?)
2. Connection questions (e.g., How is this problem different from/ similar to problems that have already been solved?)
3. Strategy questions (e.g., What strategies are appropriate for solving this problem and why?)

4. Reflection questions (e.g., Does this make sense? Why am I stuck?)

Ciardiello and McPherson believe that question generation is a skill that should be taught to students. Metacognition is embedded in this type of thinking process due to the fact that, "Research shows that self-questioning is the most effective monitoring and regulating strategy of all the various metacognitive strategies" (Ciardiello, 1998, p. 3). Ciardiello further posits that, "Generating questions is a guide that supports learners as they develop internal cognitive processes" (Ciardiello, 1998, p. 3). Costa (2008) states that the "self-generation of questions facilitates comprehension" (p. 222).

When we discuss student-generated questions, we are looking at the importance of students being able to generate thought provoking, higher level questions. Ciardiello's research shows that few students do that without explicit instruction in the skill of question generation. Ciardiello (1998) also indicates that students must be trained to develop and ask "knowledge-seeking" and "hypothesis-generating" questions. These types of questions don't have one correct or expected response and could be viewed as an essential question, leading to more questioning and triggering discussion. We know that generating thought-provoking questions is a metacognitive skill that requires explicit instruction, but how do classroom teachers go about providing instruction in the area of good question generation?

Cardiello (1998) states that often students don't have the background skills needed to generate Meta-Q questions. In order to deal with this deficiency, Cardiello developed an instructional model that teaches students how to generate questions at various levels of cognition, in three phases, and four specific types of questions; "memory-based, convergent, divergent, and evaluative." Cardiello developed TeachQuest, with the teacher providing explicit instruction, modeling and reinforcement in the skill of question generation. He called this step in question-generation instruction, TeachQuest because the teacher is the main focus at this point. Manzo's ReQuest (1969) model for reciprocal questioning served as the catalyst for Cardiello's work at the next step of instruction in student-generated questioning. The work of both Cardiello (1998) and Manzo (1969) serves as the springboard for the question-generation teaching presented in this work.

It is important to note that each specific type of question has merit and a place in instruction. The "memory-based" or factual question will most likely live forever in classrooms. Factual questions provide immediate feedback and aid in a quick checking for understanding. Many teachers over use the factual question, but the goal of Meta-Q is assist teachers in moving beyond factual questions and adding other question types of questions to their repertoire. Some examples of factual questions are:

- Where did Lewis and Clark begin their journey to explore the western territory of the United States?
- Who was the president of the United States at the time of Lewis and Clark's expedition?
- What was the name of the female guide who assisted Lewis and Clark on their expedition?

One can readily see that these types of questions have a correct answer. The questions themselves don't lead to additional questioning, nor do they provoke the learner to engage in more complex thinking. Factual questioning enables the teacher to determine whether or not the student remembers the information at that specific time. One can't assume that the content has been "learned" and is indeed in long-term memory, but only that the student remembered the information at the time of answering the question.

Convergent questions are also considered to be at a lower cognitive level and the responses are expected to fall within a specific range in order to be accurate. There is indeed a correct answer to a convergent question, but the answer is not as narrow as that of a factual question. When considering the definition of the word "convergent," one can conclude that the convergent question would require informational segments to "come together" to form a response. Examples of convergent questions are:

- Why did the president want to have someone explore the newly acquired western territory?
- Why was the journey of Lewis and Clark difficult?
- What provisions did Lewis and Clark need to have with them for the journey?

A divergent question is a question type that requires higher level cognitive processes and does not have one correct answer. Divergent questions promote creative thinking and often lead to additional questioning. Teachers sometimes shy away from divergent questioning because they can't anticipate students' responses. The concern for loosing control of the classroom environment or an inappropriate student response contributes to this hesitance to use divergent questioning. The focus on high-stakes testing also provides teachers with the rationale to avoid this type of classroom activity. Divergent questioning requires time: time for students to respond to the questions and broaden responses of their peers. Often teachers assume that they can't take the necessary time to pose divergent questions, not considering that by increasing their students' thinking capacity they increase learning, achievement and test scores. Examples of divergent questions are:

- If Meriwether Lewis were to have written a letter to his family back home in Virginia, what kinds of things that he encountered on his expedition would he have written about?
- Would the expedition of Lewis and Clark have been more or less difficult than the voyage of Christopher Columbus?
- How would the development of the United States been different if Lewis and Clark hadn't made their historic journey?

Evaluative questions require thinking at the highest cognitive level. The responses include consideration of relationships, similarities and differences, or value. The respondent calls upon his or her own frame of reference to make judgments and justify the decision making. Examples of evaluative questions are:

- What similarities and differences exist between the expedition of Lewis and Clark and Ponce de Leon? Christopher Columbus?
- How did the United States benefit from the expedition of Lewis and Clark?
- What positives and negatives can you identify in the exploration of the western territory?

Now that the various types of questions have been discussed, let's look at the steps involved in training students to ask Meta-Q type questions. For the purposes of this work, the focus will be on the development of divergent and/or evaluative questions. Cardiello (1998) suggests three phases in this instruction: "identifying divergent thinking questions, classifying divergent thinking questions, and generating divergent thinking questions."

STEP 1—IDENTIFICATION

As with any effective instruction, it is critical for students to recognize how they will benefit from being able to generate higher level questions and guided to the realization of the rationale and usefulness of the generation of higher-level questions. Teachers need to be prepared to assist students in the discovery of the higher level cognitive processes and how various question types align with the cognitive levels: i.e., analysis, synthesis, and evaluation. When beginning the instruction in the generation of higher-level questions, students should be permitted to work in small groups in order to collaborate and share thoughts about divergent questions. The term "divergent" needs to be explained and discussed with the class. Students need to understand that a divergent question will not have one correct answer, but rather will require the respondent to think deeply and broadly about the topic or issue at hand. Ask students in their groups to discuss what a divergent question might look like. What characteristics would they look for in divergent questions? Are there any critical words that could indicate divergent questions? Cardiello (1998) includes the following "key words" that could be provided to students: "if ... then ... "; "suppose that ..."; "imagine ..."; " predict ...". When the teacher observes that the students can identify a divergent question, it is time to move to the next step.

STEP 2—CLASSIFICATION

The process of analyzing and classifying questions sets the stage for generating questions. Students should be given sample questions and provided an opportunity to work in small groups to determine the cognitive level of the questions. *Are these questions asking you to analyze, synthesis, or evaluate something?* Provide students with cues for the various cognitive levels in order to guide and support this step in the progression. Examples are categorize, compare, contrast, relate to, distinguish, assess, determine, discriminate, or prioritize.

After the small groups have had the opportunity to complete this process, discuss with the whole group why specific questions would fall into the various categories. This provides and opportunity for students to be engaged in further exploring what a divergent question is and the characteristics that is possesses. This step also provides students with additional engagement with the thinking process. They will be required to use metacognitive skills to analyze the types of questions in their own minds.

STEP 3—GENERATION

The teacher should first model how a divergent question is generated. Selecting a passage from the students' text is a good place to begin. The teacher think-aloud strategy would be effective at this point of instruction. (Please refer to Chapter 3, exploring the teacher think-aloud strategy.)

After modeling the generation of several divergent questions based upon the students' text, give the small groups an opportunity to develop their own divergent questions based upon selected text passages. Students should be encouraged to try to use some of the words provided in the classification step; categorize, compare, contrast, relate to, distinguish, assess, determine, discriminate, or prioritize, as a starting point. The small group generated questions should be shared and discusses with the entire group. The questions can be analyzed and evaluated to determine whether or not the criteria established for a divergent question has been met. Using text passages to provide explicit question generating instruction serves two purposes. First, the students are gaining experience in question generation and higher level thinking. Second, the content is being contemplated in a much deeper, cognitive level.

Students will receive instruction in the identification, classification and generation of divergent questions. The steps leading up to the actual generation of the divergent question provide the opportunities for metacognition. Students will mentally reflect, classify, categorize, call upon prior knowledge and self-monitor throughout the process.

The work of Hubbard and Power (1993) focused on the teacher as a researcher, however, they provide suggestions for starting the process of inquiry that can be useful in the learning phase of question generation. They suggest creating "a list of things that you wonder about in your classroom." While their work was teacher-centered, this can be changed to a student-centered task. Ask students in their small groups to brainstorm things that they are wondering about in the classroom. As a means of additional practice in question generation, these "wonderings" can then be converted into divergent questions. Provide students with the following prompts to support them in the question-generation practice phase:

- After reading the passage (listening to the lecture, participating in the class discussion),
  o I am wondering why...
  o I am wondering how...
  o I am wondering what would happen if...
  o I am wondering how John's comment supports Mary's statement?
  o I am wondering how this compares to...

The classroom environment must be a nonthreatening atmosphere where student are confident that their questions will be respected and valued (Christenbury & Kelly, 1983).

Goodman (2010) developed what he calls Constructivist Action Learning Teams (CALT). An integral part of the CALT process is the development of the critical query. Goodman states, "Teachers provide stimulation, guidance and extrinsic motivation in order to maximize the intrinsic motivation of our students and to help them to further their understandings and knowledge" (p. 10). Goodman (2010) provides background information necessary to frame a critical query. The first step includes sharing a rationale for using critical query. We want to demonstrate some knowledge imbedded within our question. Critical query then reflects the knowledge of the conversationalist, and it furthers the discussion beyond simple reductive, 'yes' and 'no' questions (Goodman, 2010). The objective of the critical query is to move students beyond a simple "yes" or "no" response and lead to a conversation that is more intellectual and requiring critical and analytical thinking. The CALT group members work together, forming the critical queries and engaging in discussions that demonstrate deep meaning and understanding. Goodman (2010) further notes, "As present and future educators, it is incumbent upon us to teach emerging adults to see that over-generalizations are invalid and that the answers to important questions are not "Yes" or "No", but are complexities of responses belonging rightfully upon a continuum ranging widely across a spectrum of culturally-driven and diverse possibilities. Questions like, "As a nation, what should we do to reverse global warming?" are not answered with simple solutions" p. 11. The critical query moves the learner toward questioning, questioning, questioning. After participating in a CALT group, students should question with automaticity. They should not be satisfied with responses that don't delve deeply into content. Asking why should be second nature to the participant of the CALT process. The CALT process will be more appropriate with middle school, high school, or adult learners. When modified and adapted, it could be used with elementary aged students, but the nature of the process lends itself to being more effective with more mature learners.

Much of this chapter has been devoted to the rationale supporting questioning in the classroom. The authors have included why questioning enhances comprehension and stressed the importance of both teacher-generated and student-generated questions. One should also consider important points in the actual mechanics of effective questioning. One such point worthy of discussion is the issue of wait time. Wait time is the amount of time that the teacher waits to speak after posing a question. Wait time 1 will be discussed first.

Rowe (1986) brought the concept of wait time to the attention of educators in the 1970s. Rowe's findings showed that many teachers wait less than two seconds before calling on a student or restating the question. Her work showed that by increasing the amount of time that students had to process the question and formulate a response, positive changes came about. By increasing wait time, student responses became longer and more complex. Student interaction increased and the number of unsolicited, but appropriate student responses increased as well.

Wait time 1 is what one would term the timeframe from when the teacher poses the question until a student is called upon to respond. The question is posed by the teacher once and then the teacher is silent for approximately five seconds (longer is deemed necessary). After providing wait time 1, the teacher solicits a response from an individual student. One way to consciously use wait time 1 is to tell the students that the teacher is going to ask a question and that they will be given time to think before being asked to respond. After an appropriate wait time (counting to 5 in one's head works well), the teacher then signals to the class that they can raise their hand to respond. The signal can be whatever the teacher and the class has previously determined. This "think and signal" strategy removes the stress and pressure for students that require longer processing time. Classmates that require minimal processing time are not sitting with their hands raised making the slower student feel uncomfortable or causing them to just give up. Each student has the same amount of thinking time when the teacher uses wait time 1.

Wait time 2 is the time that the teacher remains silent after the student's response is given. Research has shown that student's responses sometimes come in bursts, thus if the teacher remains silent, the student has an opportunity to expand on his or her answer. Other students in the classroom may also build upon the response of their peer if the teacher remains silent and allows for wait time 2. Wait time 2 is often difficult to implement in the classroom. Teachers have been trained to provide immediate feedback and wait time 2 can feel very awkward to utilize. Appropriate feedback would follow after using both wait time 1 and wait time 2.

Keep in mind that wait time 1 is one of the single-most important strategies to bring about positive changes in students' responses. It requires no financial resources and can be immediately used in any classroom at any grade level. The authors are reluctant to say that it is easy to implement because if a teacher is not accustomed to using wait time, it can seem very cumbersome and difficult to employ. With careful and deliberate practice, a teacher can develop wait time skills. It requires one to consciously give students processing time prior to soliciting the response. Wait time 1 allows for students to operate in the metacognitive realm. They are given the time to think about their own thinking.

One other point in the area of the mechanics of effective questioning is so simple that the authors are reluctant to include it in this text. It sounds quite obvious, but often is not observed in classrooms. It is the equitable participation of students in the questioning and response process. It has been observed that often teachers call upon certain students more than others. Earlier in this chapter, the authors explained that questioning determines **what** students learn and **which** students do the learning. Teachers must be very careful to insure that all students have the opportunity to participate equitably in the classroom.

Final Thoughts

Questioning is a catalyst to learning. Effective instruction relies heavily on effective questioning. The authors have explored why questioning is important and how it effects teaching and learning. From the simple question eliciting recall of facts to the complex divergent question, each has an important role to contribute to the learning process. In order to be a metacognitive thinker, one must be able to answer and generate questions at various levels of complexity. This chapter has provided the background and the mechanics of effective questioning. Teachers must reflect on their own practices and take the steps necessary to include the Meta-Q suggested here into daily instruction.

REFERENCES

Christenbury, L., & Kelly, P. P. (1983). *Theory research into practice: Questioning a path to critical thinking*. Urbana, IL: ERIC Clearinghouse on Reading and Communication Skills & the National Council of Teachers of English.

Ciardiello, A. (1993). Training students to ask reflective questions. *Clearing House*, 66(5), 312-314. Retrieved from EBSCOhost.

Ciardiello, A. V. (1998). Did you ask a good question today? Alternative cognitive and metacognitive strategies. *Journal of Adolescent & Adult Literacy*, 42(3), 210-219. Retrieved from EBSCOhost.

Costa, A. L. (2008). *The school as a home for the mind: Creating mindful curriculum, instruction and dialogue* (2nd ed.). Thousand Oaks, CA: Corwin Press.

Goodman, G. (2010). Critical thinking: How good questions affect classrooms. In G. Goodman (Ed.), *Educational psychology reader: The art and science of how people learn* (p. 10-11). New York: Peter Lang.

Hubbard, R. S., & Power, B. M. (1993). *The art of classroom inquiry: A handbook for teacher-researchers*. Portsmouth, NH: Heinemann.

Hunkins, F. P. (1995). *Teaching thinking through effective questioning* (2nd ed.). Boston, MA: Christopher-Gordon Publishers.

Manzo, A. (1969). ReQuest: A method for improving reading comprehension through reciprocal questioning. *Journal of Reading*, 12, 123-126.

McPherson, F. (2001). Mempowered: Empowering your memory and mind. Available at http://www.memory-key.com/improving/strategies/study/metacognitive-questioning-and-use-worked-examples.

Rowe, M. B. (1986). Wait time: Slowing down may be a way of speeding up. *Journal of Teacher Education*, 37 (1), 43-50.

Walsh, J. A., & Sattes, B. A. (2003). *QUILT: Questioning and understanding to improve learning and thinking*. Charleston, WV: Appalachia Educational Laboratory.

Weir, C. (1998). Using embedded questions to jump-start metacognition in middle school remedial readers. *Journal of Adolescent & Adult Literacy*, 41(6), 458-467. Retrieved from EBSCOhost.

Wilen, W. W. (1987). *Questions, questioning techniques, and effective teaching*. Washington, DC, National Education Association. Retrieved from EBSCOhost.

CHAPTER NINE

Meta-S: Thinking while Studying

Kolencik/Hillwig

"First we hold their hand. Then we let them walk ahead, still within our sight. Next, we let them go around the corner, still within the sound of our voice. Finally, we let them go…"

Dr. Shelia Hillwig

The authors have presented various strategies to prepare for learning. These strategies for the most part focus on learning in the classroom. While the preparation for learning in the classroom is important, it is only part of the process. Effective learners not only apply the metacognitive strategies in the classroom, but ideally attain self-assessment, and self-directed utilization of strategies. Our goal as educators is to facilitate the learning until the learner is proficient enough to apply the strategies on his or her own, as needed. This chapter focuses on strategies that assist the student in preparing to learn through utilizing study skills.

Effective learners should have a repertoire of study skills to draw upon in a variety of learning situations. Keep in mind that the ultimate goal is for the learner to KNOW when to use these strategies. Study strategies are diverse and don't work in every context. For example, reading for information acquisition won't work in a literature course and won't work if students are supposed to critically evaluate an article. But, students who have learned only the strategy of reading to pass a quiz on the information will not go beyond this strategy. Study strategies don't automatically transfer into other domains. Students need to know that they have choices about which strategies to employ in different contexts. Students who learn study strategies in one course need to apply those same strategies in contexts other than that where it was first learned.

Metacognitive learners self-monitor, using the appropriate strategy when needed and they monitor their application of study strategies. Metacognitive awareness of one's learning processes is as important as monitoring one's learning of the course content. An essential component of metacognition is employing study strategies to reach a goal, self-assessing one's effectiveness in reaching that goal, and then self-regulating in response to the self-assessment.

One pitfall for teachers is the assumption that the learners have already developed the study skills needed to be successful. It is shown in research that few teachers purposefully teach study strategies because they believe that the students will have innately developed study skills (McKeachie, 1988). Simpson and Nist ((1990) state that it takes time to teach explicit use of strategies; but not only the use of the strategy, but when to use a particular strategy as well. They further state that instruction in study strategies "should be explicit and direct" and should include five features: "(a) strategy descriptions; (b) discussions of why the strategy should be learned and its importance; (c) think-alouds, models, and examples of how the strategy is used, including the processes involved and when and where it is appropriate to apply the strategy; (d) explanations as to when and where it is appropriate to apply the strategy; and (e) suggestions for monitoring and evaluation whether the strategy is working and what to do if it is not." Instructors should design guided practice where students use the strategies on authentic course tasks; not unrelated, isolated tasks, and provide feedback.

In this segment, we will assume nothing and present some very basic strategies for students to employ. Research indicates that when teachers set

high standards and stress the importance of good study skills, students achieve at higher levels. We will examine:
- Study Environments
- Organization
- Engaged Study
- Note Taking
- Textbook Skills
- Test Taking

Study Environments

Setting, light, sound, and temperature are some of the elements of study environments. Everything that surrounds the learner is part of the study environment. Teachers must provide instruction on creating the study environment.

SETTING

The setting is where the student does the studying and can be anywhere, indoors or outside. The setting can be in various rooms in the student's home or in school. It may include a desk or a table. Some students need a formal setting while others may feel that they are more successful in an informal study environment. Many students believe that they are more successful with the television blasting, or listening to music. The teacher's role is to help them actually self-assess to determine where they are most successful when studying. Teachers should direct students to ask themselves where they are able to best concentrate, or where they are most alert.

LIGHT

The amount of light can affect one's ability to concentrate. Some students need a brightly lit room while others are sensitive to glare and study better in a room with softer lighting. Eye strain can occur if there is insufficient light, or dim lighting might cause the learner to actually fall asleep. Students need to determine the lighting they need to be most successful in their environment.

SOUND

The amount and type of sound in the study environment can have a powerful affect on one's ability to think and remember. Some learners need absolute quiet, being easily distracted by noise. Other learners may be more successful with music or other sounds that actually disguise distracting background noises. The important thing to note is the fact that the learners must be able to recognize their individual learning preferences. Generally, studying is easier in a quiet place with minimal interruptions. In the age of constant communication, it is a good idea to suggest that cell phones be turned off or placed in another room at home. Constant incoming texts and instant messages do not create an environment with minimal interruptions.

Some students believe that they study best in front of the television because it provides background noise that is beneficial. Generally speaking, the television is not the best media for background sound because it provides visuals and a story line too. Research has shown that one's brain is able to process only one thing at a time (Wolfe, 2001). If the television is on and the learner is trying to process the story line and study at the same time, it does not work. Stress to learners that a separate time should be scheduled to watch television apart from study time.

TEMPERATURE

It is hard to stay alert and focused when one is physically uncomfortable. If the room is too hot it is easy to become distracted and maybe even sleepy. When it is too cold it can be just as hard to concentrate. Help learners determine what they individually need to be able to do their best work. Temperature is an important element in the study environment.

Most learners will benefit from these guidelines. The key here is "most". It is important for the learner to self-assess and determine the study environment that is best for him or her, but generally speaking the following points will contribute to a good study environment.

- Find a quiet place.
- Have good lighting.
- Sit at a table or desk.
- Find a chair that requires you to sit up straight.
- Use your good location each time you study.

The following study environment "road map" will help direct your students toward the development of good study habits (Table 9.1).

Study Environment Road Map

Travelers use maps to help them get from one place to another. This study environment road map will help you move toward the study environment that is best suited for you. Ask yourself the following questions. The answers will guide you in the direction that you need to go in order to be a successful, self-monitoring learner.

Do I study best in a private area of my home?
Do I study best in the same place each time?
Do I study best in an area that is uncluttered and free from distractions?
Do I have a study area with all of my necessary materials organized and readily available?
Where am I best able to concentrate and stay focused until my assignments are completed?
Do bright lights help me stay alert when I study or do they bother my eyes?
Do I concentrate better when it is absolutely quiet or with some quiet background sounds?
Am I more comfortable studying when the room temperature is warm or cool?

Consider each of the answers you provided and map out how you are going to create the best study environment for you. Your study environment may be different from your best friend's. Everyone has a study and learning style that is unique. It is important for you to be able to recognize the environment that you need to create in order to be successful.

Table 9.1 Study Environment Road Map

Organization

It is important for teachers to instruct students in the art of being organized. For some this will come naturally, but for those that have not acquired organizational skills, this is an important dimension of being a metacognitive learner. We will examine two facets of organization; organizing self and organizing time.

ORGANIZING SELF

Provide the students with the following tips on organizing themselves:

- Always write assignments in an agenda or planner when the assignment is given. Don't wait and try to remember, do it when it is assigned. (Students need to understand that the agenda or planner is an important tool for everyone. If adults in various professions were surveyed and asked how they remember to do everything expected of them each week, they would most likely respond that they write things down. Perhaps they use a written agenda or keep appointments and tasks in a PDA or BlackBerry. They write notes and jot things down to help keep themselves organized.)

- Have a folder or notebook for each class. Keep assignments, returned tests, projects, homework, and all important papers for the class in the notebook or folder. With this system of organization, you will always know where the papers for each class are located and nothing will get lost.

- Chose notebooks or folders of different colors for each class. Using red for science, blue for math, and another different color for each additional class, minimizes the risk of taking the wrong folder or notebook to the class. If the folders are all the same color you need to look at the title or the contents inside to see what you need. By color coding the folders you save time and are sure to take the correct folder each and every time.

- Clean out your backpack, locker, and desks (at home and at school) weekly. Get rid of unneeded **junk**. If something will help you study for a test in a specific class at a later time, place it in the folder for that class. Throw away everything else that isn't useful.

- Plan for the next day before you go to bed. Put everything that you will need to take to school together. Think about the classes that you will have and gather all of the necessary items. Do you need to return a library book or take clothes for gym class? Put the items in the same place every night so that you know exactly where everything is in the morning when you are getting ready to go to school

- When preparing to leave school at the end of the day, don't guess about what you will need to take home with you. Take the time to look at your planner or agenda and make sure you take the materials that you will need to study and complete assignments. It is difficult to accomplish tasks when perhaps the most important book or paper is in your locker or desk.

Help students set organization goals. Encourage them to choose one of the tips provided and actually write a weekly goal. Giving them a framework for the written goal will make goal writing easier. Help them to develop their individual goals and write them in their planners or agendas. For example, *This week I will begin to* _____.

After a few weeks of working with the students on setting organizational goals, it should be easier for them to self-assess and determine the areas that still need additional attention.

Teachers must be cognizant of the need to model self-monitoring strategies, provide guidance as students begin to use the strategies, and maintain consistent expectations for the use of the self-monitoring tools. The Pennsylvania Department of Education published a document, *Starting Off Right: Resources for New Teachers* (2000), which includes several points for promoting metacognition. The section of the document that is relevant to organizing self, deals with homework tips. *Starting Off Right: Resources for New Teachers* includes these homework tips:

H – Have students use a planning calendar to write down assignment.

O – Offer ways for students to seek help in completing assignments.

M – Make sure the students are able to complete the assignment independently.

E – Establish consistent routines for homework completion early in the school year.

W – Write the assignment/directions on the board and provide students the time to copy.

O – Organize the students for the task by modeling the necessary steps to complete the assignment.

R – Remind students of due dates.

K – Keep communication open with parents and students about homework policies, required practices, expectation, and performance on homework.

While the acrostic itself is a metacognitive strategy, when reflecting on each of the associated statements, one can see the metacognition that is required of students. Each of the modeled and taught skills guides the student toward independently utilizing self-monitoring and self-regulating skills.

Middle school students may benefit from the "Reminder Checklists" (Table 9.2) suggested by Dodge (1994) in *The Study Skills Handbook: More than 75 Strategies for Better Learning*. She suggests checklists for home and school that include reminders of things that need to be accomplished at each location. An example "at home" would be "Bring lunch money", and an "at school" example is "Place in Travel Folder any notices handed out to go home." Dodge further suggests blank areas on the checklist where students can add their own unique reminders.

AT HOME

_____ Pack all homework, texts, notebooks in bookbag or backpack.

_____ Bring lunch or lunch money. (With the advent of point-of-sales crediting in school cafeterias, this might not be an item to be included in the checklist.)

_____ Place any unsigned papers in Travel Folder.

_____ Eat a good breakfast.

_____ Things that need to be done before school: _____

_____

AT SCHOOL

_____ Before packing to leave, check planner or agenda.

_____ Bring home any texts, notebooks, or other materials that will be needed.

_____ Ask the teacher about any upcoming tests or projects.

_____ Place any notices handed out in the Travel Folder to go home.

MY REMINDER CHECKLIST

1. _____

2. _____

_____

3. _____

Adapted from Dodge, 1994.

Table 9.2 Reminder Checklists

ORGANIZING TIME

Often students believe that teachers just don't understand how much work they have to do and just "pile on" homework. Once in a while that may be the case, but when students organize and manage their time wisely it is much easier for them to complete the required tasks. The following tips will assist students in organizing and managing their time:

- Be ready when you sit down to study. Have your materials in front of you and your planner or agenda open. When you have to jump up and down to get things that you need to study, you waste valuable time. Some things that you will need to consider having are pencils, pens, highlighter, paper, lined writing paper, calculator, dictionary, and a stapler. This is simply an example and not meant to be a fully inclusive list of materials needed for studying.

- Have a clock available to help you budget your time.
- Study the most difficult subject first. It is easier to work on more difficult things when you are fresh. If you begin to get tired or frustrated, go to an easier assignment and then go back and complete the more difficult work.
- If you begin to feel sleepy or distracted, take a break. Get up and get a snack, take a short walk, or something else that is active. Don't lie down and take a nap.
- Study for tests a little at a time. If you know several days in advance that you have a big test coming up, study for it for several days, a little each day. Do not cram for the test. Cramming isn't learning. The morning of the test, review your material to refresh your memory.
- This might be the hardest tip to follow, but maybe one of the most important. Don't allow yourself to get behind in any subject. If you keep up with your work daily, it will pay off in the end. It is much easier and more effective to study and work a little each day then to try to catch up. If you keep up with assignments and review each subject everyday, you won't feel overwhelmed right before a test.
- Help students set time-organization goals. Encourage them to choose one of the tips provided and actually write a weekly goal. Giving them a framework for the written goal will make goal writing easier. Help them to develop their individual time-management goals and write them in their planners or agendas. For example, *This week I will begin to* _____.

After a few weeks of working with the students on setting time-organizational goals, it should be easier for them to self-assess and determine the areas that still need additional attention.

Most learners will benefit from the following time-management and organizational guidelines:

- Write down all assignments and when they are due. Try to estimate how long it will take to complete each assignment.
- Write down when tests are scheduled.
- Check off completed assignments.
- Write down special instructions.
- Ask questions if you are confused.

Some students may need to have time management tools provided to them in order to make best use of their time. Provide students with a blank schedule and encourage them to use it to budget out-of-school time (Table 9.3).

Time	Monday	Tuesday	Wednesday	Thursday	Friday
3:00-3:30					
3:30-4:00					
4:00-4:30					
4:30-5:00					
5:00-5:30					
5:30-6:00					
6:00-6:30					
6:30-7:00					
7:00-7:30					
7:30-8:00					
8:00-8:30					
8:30-9:00					
9:00-9:30					
9:30-10:00					

Table 9.3 My Weekly Schedule

After a few weeks of using the suggested schedule, ask students to reflect upon how they are using their time. This self-assessment of time management will help students determine whether or not they are using their time wisely. They may also observe that they are postponing their homework and studying until late in the evening. If they seem to be struggling to complete assignments and prepare for tests, this may be one explanation. Suggest that they try to begin their assignments earlier in the evening when they are less fatigued.

For long-term projects or reports that require multiple weeks to complete, students need to be aware of the tasks required to complete the assignment and the time required. A blank, weekly calendar (Table 9.4) should be provided to students in order for them to budget the time necessary to complete the assignment. The "Independent Study Ladder" (Table 9.5) will assist students in the steps needed to complete a long-term assignment. "Keeping a Research Log" (Table 9.6) will provide students the opportunity monitor their progress on long-term projects.

Students need to be instructed how to plan for completion of a long-term project. Keep in mind, for some students, this may be the first time that they are being asked to complete an assignment such as this. If that is the case, they may not have developed the organizational skills needed to know how to approach such a task.

Write the tasks that you will complete each day of each week from the time the assignment is given until the assignment is completed.

Sunday	Monday	Tuesday	Wednesday	Thursday	Friday	Saturday

Table 9.4 Long-Term Project/Report Planner Calendar

Independent Study Ladder

Finish
Did you GET IDEAS for your next project/report?
EVALUATE your work.
SHARE your finished project.
Choose your METHOD FOR REPORTING your findings.
Start digging into those RESOURCES.
GATHER the MATERIALS that you will need.
SHARE your plan with your teacher.
Make a PLAN.
Choose a TOPIC of interest to you.
START

Developed by Vicki Shoemaker, Kiski Area School District, 2006

Table 9.5 Independent Study Ladder

Keeping a Research Log

Purpose: To keep an orderly record of your activities and to check your progress.
Materials Needed: Log sheets, note cards
Procedures: Record all activities that you do for this assignment.
Product: A completed log to turn in with finished assignment, or to monitor your progress.

Sample Log
Project Title:_____
Name: _____ Date:_____

Self-check: Tell what you accomplished today.
Example: Today I was assigned to be in the group on creating a calendar and I used the Internet to look up TIME.

Summary: Tell the results of your day's research.
Example: I learned that the word MONTH comes from the word MOON.

Questions: Write any questions which came into your mind as you were doing today's activities. These can be questions about your task, your role in the group (if a group project), the information you found, or any other concerns.
Example: How is knowing that the word month came from the word moon going to help us with our calendar?

Plan: Organize your plans for tomorrow. List specific tasks you want to accomplish.
Example: Tomorrow I will search the for information on the Julian calendar and I will take notes on my findings.

Table 9.6 Keeping a Research Log

Engaged Study

Teachers spend a great deal of time planning instruction that is engaging and keeps students actively involved in the learning. Students are asked to *create, tell, draw, list, imagine, write,* and a myriad of other active, engaging terms. We then send students out of our classrooms and ask them to independently study. Unless we provide students with the tools needed to help them with engaged study, they embark upon a session of passive review of notes or looking over the text. Passive studying isn't very effective for many students. Instructing students in engaged-study strategies will result in more successful independent study sessions. Students should be expected to use the same engaged behaviors when they are working outside of the classroom. *Create, tell, draw, list, imagine,* and *write* are examples of the things that students need to be encouraged to use when independently working. Table 9.7 outlines strategies for engaged study.

Teachers need to take time in class to teach students the art of engaged

---

Engaged Study

When I study, I should *tell*. Some things that I could do are:
- Talk to myself, out loud, and explain the material I am studying.
- Tell another person what it is that I am learning. Pretend that I am the teacher and teach someone else the information or concept.
- With a recorder or webcam, I could record myself explaining the topic and then listen to my recording to determine whether I covered all of the material thoroughly.

When I study, I should *create*. Some things that I could do are:
- Create a diagram, a chart, a list, or a graphic organizer that tests my memory of the information on the topic. I then will use the textbook and my notes to check my work.
- Create flashcards with vocabulary, main ideas and key words. Write the definitions or explanations on the back.
- Create memory aids, like mnemonic devices to help me remember.
- Create an outline of the topic from memory and then check the outline with the textbook and notes to ensure accuracy.

When I study, I should *imagine*. Some things that I could do are:
- Try to "see" in my mind any charts, graphs or timelines that the teacher used in class.
- Imagine what a particular character looked like and "see" in my mind what that character did.

Some ways that I can be sure that I use engaged study are:
    When I am studying I will try to_____.

(Adapted from Dodge, 1994).

Table 9.7 Engaged Study

---

study. Discuss with students some of the strategies of engaged study listed in Table 9.7. As a class, brainstorm other engaged study strategies. Students will no doubt come up with other ideas for engagement that are not listed here. List the strategies on a poster or other display in the classroom. As new strategies are identified, add them to the chart. Ask students to identify one of the engaged study strategies that they will attempt to use in their independent study sessions. Allow for time in class for follow-up discussions. Ask students to evaluate the strategy and reflect on its effectiveness. It's important to note that not every strategy will be effective for every student. Differences in learning styles will effect whether or not a strategy will benefit a student while using engaged study. A critical component of metacognition is self-monitoring and self-regulating. Students need to develop the ability to recognize the strategies that work best for their own individual learning and studying styles. To encourage self-monitoring in students, the self-evaluation instrument in Table 9.8 could be introduced as part of the follow-up discussion.

Study Self-Evaluation

Place an X on the line if the task was completed.

_____ I studied in a quiet place.

_____ I made sure to turn off things that distract me; TV, cell phone, music.

_____ I used my agenda or planner to make sure that daily assignments were completed.

_____ I completed all of my assignments for every class.

_____ I organized my study area, notebooks, desk, or folders and disposed of things that I didn't need and placed things I need to keep in a special place.

_____ I studied the most difficult subjects first.

_____ I tried to study earlier in the evening/day.

_____ I paid careful attention in class.

_____ I took notes during class lectures and discussions.

_____ I took notes from my textbook.

_____ I used engaged study strategies to prepare for tests.

_____ I reviewed notes from each class every day.

A new strategy that I tried this week was:_____.

The new strategy (worked well) (didn't work well) because:_____.

I am most proud of:_____.

I need to work harder on: _____.

My goal for next week is:_____.

Adapted from Dodge, 1994.

Table 9.8 Study Self-Evaluation

Note Taking

Students must be instructed in the art of note taking. Note taking is important because it will help students summarize lectures and textbook readings, help them prepare for exams, requires students to be actively engaged as a reader and listener, and improves students' memory skills. Note taking can be broken down into two categories: note taking from textbook readings and note taking from class lectures and discussions. Both categories of note taking will be investigated and tips for promoting the skill to students will be discussed.

Note taking in any form brings about positive results in students. Note taking aids retention and comprehension, helps students become more organized and requires students to process information (Dodge, 1994). Teachers must model various forms of note taking and provide students the opportunity to practice each several times with teacher support. After ample guided practice, students should be able to implement the form of note taking that will best meet the needs of the assignment. It should be noted that note taking in this text is not referring to the student copying information from the board or computer screen. Note taking is referring to the student receiving information, processing that information, summarizing, paraphrasing, determining main ideas, and notating the information in some form.

NOTE TAKING FROM THE TEXTBOOK

Before taking notes from the textbook, some preliminary instruction should be provided to students. One strategy that students can use when reading a textbook is Robinson's, study method, SQ3R (Robinson, 1961). Instructing students to use the SQ3R method when reading textbooks results in students being engaged in the reading, comprehension enhanced and note taking after using SQ3R will help them prepare for tests (Dodge, 1994). One way in which SQ3R supports note taking is by guiding students toward the identification of main ideas, a critical aspect of note taking. Let's look at what makes up the SQ3R study method (Robinson, 1961).

SURVEY—Take a few minutes scanning chapter headings, captions, graphs, charts, boldface or italicized words, and section/chapter questions to look for main ideas and predict the chapter content. Read the summary at the end of the chapter, if provided.

QUESTION—Purposefully write questions that you believe will be answered in the reading. Sometimes it is easier to turn chapter subheadings into questions to create a purpose for your reading.

READ—Actively read each section to answer the question/s you created in the previous step.

RECITE—After reading a section, pause, look away and try to answer in your own words, the question you created for that section and give examples when possible. If you are unable to answer the question, look at the section again, turn away and try to answer the question. From memory, make very brief notes of key phrases in outline form. Repeat steps; Question, Read, and Review on each headed section of the chapter—turn each heading into a question, read to answer the question, recite the answer, and jot down cue phrases. Read in this way until finished with the chapter. Recitation helps fix information in your memory.

REVIEW—When finished with the chapter, review your notes, and recite major points under each heading to test your memory. This memory check can be done by physically covering your notes and trying to recall main points. Then uncover each major point and try to recall subpoints or supporting details. The table of contents and subject headings in chapters are usually the same. Use the table of contents to test your memory of chapter content. Frequent self-testing helps improve memory, confidence, and ability to retrieve information during exams.

The Cornell note taking framework can be used with the SQ3R method very effectively. This note taking format was developed by Cornell University professor Walter Paulk and can be incorporated into taking notes from the text reading assignments and class lectures (Keeley, 1997). An example of the Cornell note taking format is presented in Table 9.9.

Subject:_____ Note Taking_____

Date:_____

MAIN IDEAS

Cornell note taking

DETAILS

- Can be used to develop an outline of the text reading assignment, or class lecture.
- Arranged by main ideas in the left column and the supporting details in the right column.
- Helps students determine main ideas
- As many supporting details as needed can be included
- Notes from text reading assignment or class lectures are created in a sequential and orderly manner.
- Is more effectively used with material presented in a sequential order.
- Provides the student with the opportunity to write a summary of what was learned.
- Can be used as vocabulary development aid:
1. Words in boldface print, unfamiliar words or concepts are noted in the left column..
2. Explanations and definitions are noted in the right column.

Concept Map or other appropriate graphic organizer

- Can help students "map out" concepts and information presented in text reading assignment or class lecture.
- Main idea is at the core or the map and details and sub-details stem from the main idea.
- Difficult to include extensive details
- Works best in class lectures that don't follow a sequential order.
- May need to be followed up with Cornell or some other type of more structured note taking method.

Illustrations for younger students

- Younger students can use an illustration for their main idea
- Teachers will need to model and provide guided practice for identifying the main idea and determining supporting details.
- Can be used for note taking from a class lecture, activity or a reading selection.
- Can be the introduction to note taking for younger students.

Summary: Students can provide the summary of the text reading assignment or class lecture by paraphrasing and combining main ideas.

Adapted from Bucks County Community College, 1997.

Table 9.9 Cornell Note Taking

NOTE TAKING FROM CLASS LECTURES

Middle school and high school students are often required to take notes during a class lecture or discussion. It is important for students to have note-taking tools available to be able to efficiently complete this task. To be a successful note taker, students need to be able to recognize key ideas or main ideas in the lecture. This will prevent them from trying to script every word that the teacher says. Students should be instructed to do the following when taking notes in class:

- Listen carefully to what the teacher is saying.
- Jot down key points or main ideas and be careful to include:
  o Any information the teacher writes on the board or computer screen.
  o Any information that is repeated or strongly emphasized by the teacher.
  o Any information that the teacher specifically refers to in the text.
- Use key words, not complete sentences
- Leave out "little" words such as "a", "an", "the", "to", and "in".
- Divide the page into two columns. Take notes in one column and leave the other column blank. You can go back and add needed information or clarification in the blank column along side your notes from class.
- Write quickly using abbreviations (Table 9.10).

Abbreviation Chart

SYMBOLS		A FEW LETTERS ONLY	
#	number	amt	amount
%	percent	assoc	association
$	money	b/c	because
+	plus and more	bio	biology, biography
-	negative, not, no	cont	continue/d
=	equal	def	definition
>	greater than	eg., ex.	for example
<	less than	etc.	also, and so forth
≠	unequal, does not equal	govt	government
≥	equal to or greater than	info	information
≤	equal to or less than	intro	introduction
⊠	to or toward	pp	pages
⊠	away from	re	regarding, about
@	at, per, each	s/t	sometimes
		w/	with
		w/o	without

Table 9.10 Abbreviation Chart

The abbreviation chart (Table 9.10) offered is a sampling of some of the note taking abbreviations available. With the inundation of texting, many students already have acquired an extensive repertoire of texting words and symbols that can be used in note taking as well. Help your students make the connection between their texting language and their note taking. They may be more enthusiastic about taking notes in class if they consider it to be an extension of their texting culture.

Preliminary work in helping students identify the main idea or key words is a critical component to note taking. Teachers can instruct students in the skill of identification of main ideas by selecting a short passage from the text and actually teaching a mini-lesson on finding the main idea or key words. This instructional activity lends itself well to the Think-Pair-Share format. After modeling identification of the main idea and supporting details, provide a second passage from the text and permit the students to work with their partners. In pairs students should be instructed to identify the main idea and then to decide which statements provide supporting details. Some visual learners may benefit from using a graphic web when completing this assignment.

Students should not be permitted to highlight as a note taking tool until instruction in main idea identification has taken place. Many students tend to highlight everything, which defeats the purpose of highlighting in the first place. Model how highlighting key words and main ideas should be done and provide students the opportunity to practice this skill several times before asking them to do so independently. When considering that note taking is intended to aid comprehension, increase retention, and improve metacognition then highlighting must be thought of as modified note taking.

Highlighting is a study skill that is used effectively with all grade levels. First graders can be instructed to highlight key words when faced with solving mathematics word problems. The same first graders can highlight the key words in a sentence, laying the foundation for more complex thinking tasks in higher grades. The important thing for teachers to remember is that the skill of highlighting must be taught. Students will not innately know how to best use this study strategy without instruction.

Textbook Skills

Students in all types of classrooms are given textbooks and often they have **never** been taught how to actually read the text. Teachers must instruct their students in the process necessary to read and take notes from a textbook. The following summarizes some strategies that students can use to read and take notes from their textbooks.

Students should first determine the note taking strategy that they think would be best for the specific lesson. Students may wish to use the Two Column method or the Skeletal Outline method described previously. After selecting the note taking strategy to use, students should be instructed in these basic steps:

Before you begin to read you should:

1. Read the title of the chapter and each heading and subheading.
2. Read the opening paragraph of the chapter.
3. Read the first section summary.
4. Preview all pictures, captions, graphs, and charts.
5. Read the questions at the end of the first section or turn the heading into a question.
   - Heading: The Process of Photosynthesis
   - Question: What is photosynthesis and what are the steps of photosynthesis?

Additional before reading strategies:

- Instruct students write down what they already know about the subject of the chapter or section and briefly discuss their responses.
- Ask someone to present an oral summary of the text reading from the previous class. This could also be done as a Think-Pair-Share activity in order to engage all of the students.
- Ask students some interesting questions that will be answered in the reading assignment.
- Take a poll on some of the issues addressed in the reading assignment.
- Emphasize the interest, usefulness, and fit in the content sequence of the chapter.
- Ask students to make a text-to-self connection. Text-to-self connections are effective in accessing prior knowledge and are considered to be one of the scientifically-based, effective practices.
- Use the SQ4R study method when reading new material.

During reading you should:

1. Chunk or break the reading into smaller sections. Paragraphs are recommended chunks.
2. Read the paragraph doing the following:
   a. Look up new vocabulary.
   b. Break down difficult sentences into smaller parts.

    c. Refer to tables, pictures, charts, and diagrams.

    d. Attend to important words and ideas.

3. Stop at the end of the paragraph.

4. Mentally summarize important details.

Additional during reading strategies:

- Answer teacher-provided questions.
- Ask and answer student-generated questions.
- Produce an outline or concept map.

After reading you should:

1. Think about what you have just read.

2. Using your chosen note taking strategy, record the vocabulary and key points in your own words.

3. Backtrack and reread difficult parts.

- Make personal connections with the text before, during, and after reading.
- Continue chunking, reading, and note taking as described above.
- At the end of the selection, review your question(s) and recite and answer aloud. If you are uncertain of an answer(s) review the selection.

Additional after reading strategies:

- Write summaries of each section in the chapter.
- Revisit the SQ4R method: Survey the text, formulate questions, read, record notes, recite, and reflect.
- Write notes that elaborate on the textbook.
- Connect the reading to a past lesson or to prior knowledge.
- Compare/contrast with another reading
- Critique/evaluate the reading
- Apply the chapter content to a scenario or case.
- Write a self-assessment of your understanding of the reading.
  - o Did any of the parts of the text confuse me? What did I do when this happened?
  - o How did this passage make me feel? What in my life might have contributed to my feeling the way that I do? Why?

The strategies described for note taking while reading the textbook, can be used without requiring students to actually take notes. The important points before, during and after reading are vital for students to use in order to increase comprehension, aid retention and ultimately, transfer.

Test Taking

Students all over the world prepare for taking tests. It is important to provide students with strategies to make the task of test taking easier to manage. There are some very basic steps that students should use regularly when preparing for a test. Provide students with the following tips:

- Keep up with your assignments.
- Practice early when you know in advance that you will be having a test.
- Break studying into chunks and study or review a little each day.
- Know what to study:
    o Facts, vocabulary, general concepts
    o Notes from lectures or the textbook
    o Review study guides provided by the teacher
    o Pay attention in class to any oral reviews the teacher conducts
- Review the following the night before the testing day:
    o Main headings
    o Vocabulary, facts such as people, places, events, dates
    o Text/lecture notes
    o Review/study guides
    o Pictures, captions, charts, graphs, diagrams
    o Questions at the end of each section and chapter
- Never cram!!

It is also to provide the students with strategies to help them retrieve information that they have previously learned. The chapter on Thinking with Mnemonics discusses this in more detail, but some basic, simple strategies to trigger memory are provided here:

- Rhymes
    o In 1492, Columbus sailed the ocean blue.
- Acrostics (silly sentence)
    o To memorize the order of mathematical operations:
        - **P**arenthesis, **E**xponents, **M**ulitiplication, **D**ivision, **A**ddition, **S**ubtraction *Please excuse my dear, Aunt Sally.*
- Acronyms (wacky words)
    o To memorize the spectrum of colors:
        - **R**ed, **O**range, **Y**ellow, **G**reen, **B**lue, **I**ndigo, **V**iolet *Roy G Biv*
- Charting (to compare and contrast ideas) (see Table 9.11)

Charting			
	BLOODED	BREATHING	REPRODUCTION
Fish	Cold	Gills	External
Amphibians	Cold	Gills, lungs	External
Reptiles	Cold	Lungs	External
Birds	Warm	Lungs	External
Mammals	Warm	Lungs	Internal

Table 9.11 Charting

- Visual Emphasis (highlight, circle, box, or color segments of information)
  - To learn the process of photosynthesis, highlight the key words:
    - Green plants combine *water* and *carbon dioxide* and *energy* from sunlight to *make food.*
- Visualization (Draw a picture or visualize something that helps you to recall the information at a later time.)
  - To recall the definition of insuperable, unable to overcome, you could imagine a can of soup trying to jump over a wall. You could actually draw a picture of that image to aid retention.
  - To learn facts such as capitals of states or countries, you could associate words and images. An example is Brussels, Belgium could be associated with Brussels sprouts sitting on a Belgium waffle.
- Association (Associate facts and use that association in a phrase, a sentence a rhyme, or a story.)
  - To learn the capitals of the U.S. states:
    - Juneau, Alaska—Too cold to go to *Alaska* except in *June*
    - Hartford, Connecticut—*Connected hearts*
    - Springfield, Illinois—You can't *spring* out of bed if you're *ill.*
- Word linking (Use word linking for form association that link one idea to the next in order to be able to remember information in a certain sequence.)
  - To memorize the names of the inert elements on the Periodic Table, Helium, Neon, Argon, Krypton, Xenon, and Radon, make up a word link as shown here:

- Helium-Helium balloon
- Neon- The helium balloon is holding up a colored neon sign.
- Argon-Associate the state of Oregon with Argon. Oregon is on the neon sign.
- Krypton-Imagine Superman on the ground under the neon sign holding kryptonite.
- Xenon-Imagine the kryptonite is refueling at an Exxon pump (looks like Xenon) and Superman is holding on to the Exxon pump.
- Radon-Imagine the xenon (Exxon pump) is zapped by a huge red ray gun (radon).

- Story linking (If the information is too long, break up the information into smaller chunks and link them together into a story.)
  o To memorize the first ten U.S. presidents the following story could be used:
    - When *Washington* cut down the cherry tree, he also cut his *Adam's* apple. Blood gushed all over his *Son, Jeff* (Jefferson). Jeff was *Mad* (Madison) at the *Money* (Monroe) fixing another *Adam's* (another Adams) apple would cost. Along came the nicer *Son, Jack* (Jackson) to help, but his *Van Burned* (Van Buren) while *Hurrying* (Harrison) to the hospital, so they just temporarily *Tied* (Tyler) a bandage around the bloody wound.

It is important to provide students with strategies to use when approaching different types of tests. Each type of test has its own "strategy of attack" and students need to know the different ways to deal with each.

Essay Questions

1. Read all of the directions.
2. Read the question highlighting key words that require relevant information and a specific type of response; describe, outline, discuss, prove, explain, list, state.
3. Questions that include these words require you to support your opinion with facts: criticize, evaluate, interpret, justify.
4. If there is more that one part to the question make sure that you number each part of the question.
5. Create a thought box, or web of related details.
6. Use your details from the web or thought box to write sentences that would answer the questions.

7. Write the essay response by following your lead sentence with supporting facts and details from the web/thought box and conclude the response by restating the lead sentence.
8. Reread your answer:
   a. Did I answer all parts of the question?
   b. Does it make sense?
   c. Is my spelling correct?
   d. Did I use proper punctuation and capitalization?

Matching Tests
1. Read all of the directions.
2. Count the choices in each column to see if they match or if there are extra choices.
3. Work the column with the explanations first, highlighting key words.
4. Think of an answer before looking at the choices.
5. Mark your choice.

Multiple-Choice Tests
1. Read all of the directions.
2. Cover up the choices below the first statement.
3. Read the statement and highlight the key words.
4. Think of an answer before looking at the choices.
5. Check the choices and mark the answer closet to the one that you thought of.
6. Be on the lookout for negatives:
   o Which is not true?
   o All of the following are true except?
   o A good way to decide on this type is to mark each one either true or false before determining the answer.

True-False Tests
1. Read all of the directions.
2. Read the first statement and highlight the key words.
3. Don't get tricked by negatives.
4. If it's true, the entire statement must be true.
5. If ANY part of the statement is false, then the entire statement is false.

Fill-in Tests

1. Read all of the directions.
2. Read the first statement highlighting key words.
3. If you know the missing part, fill it in and reread it to make certain that it makes sense.
4. If you do not know the missing part, skip it and go back to it later.
5. If you are given a word bank, make sure you copy the words/phrases correctly from the bank.
6. Cross off the words/phrases from the word bank as you use them.

Self-Monitoring

Students should be encouraged to complete self-assessments in order to monitor their own progress with study skills. The assessment in Table 9.12 can be used to guide students through the self-assessment process. Encourage students to complete the assessment multiple times, noting areas of improvement or areas requiring further development. Students can use different colored pens or pencils each time in order to more easily identify the time period in which the self-assessment is completed (Robinson, 1990).

Study Skills Self-Assessment

Reflect on your use of each of the following study skills and score yourself based on the scale:

0-I never do this.   1- I hardly ever do this.   2-I do this once in a while.
3-I usually do this.   4-I always do this.

	0	1	2	3	4
1. I scan a textbook chapter paying attention to the introduction, section headings, captions, boldface or italicized print, summaries, and questions before I actually begin to read the assigned section/s carefully.					
2. I find out what the expectations of upcoming tests are, what material will be covered, what type of test it will be and study for that specific type of test.					
3. I find out meanings of new vocabulary words used in assignments and readings.					
4. I stop while I am reading to question myself about what was just read.					
5. I talk to myself or another person about what I just read in my book.					
6. I study a little bit each day, reviewing each day's classes and add any information I may have missed.					
7. I correct mistakes and study things that I didn't get correct on tests.					
8. I write down all of my assignments and due dates in my planner or agenda and estimate how long each assignment will take me to complete.					
9. I keep my study materials, notebooks, and planner clearly organized.					
10. I study every weekday with a specific routine; in the same study area and approximately the same time of the day.					
11. I listen very attentively in class.					
12. I take notes of some type in each class every day.					

Table 9.12 Study Skills Assessment

Additionally, students should be provided a framework for metacognitive self-assessment such as:

- This week the strategy that I used that helped me the most was:_____.
- This week I put a great deal of effort into:_____.
- Because of my hard work, I am beginning to see improvement in:____
  _____.
- I feel really proud of:_____.
- I know that I need to work harder to:_____.
- One strategy that I used that didn't produce the outcome I expected was: _____.
- My goal for next week is:_____.

As stated in the introductory paragraph, our goal as educators is facilitate the learning until the learner is proficient enough to apply the strategies on their own, as needed. We have explored several strategies that can be employed in the areas of:

- Study Environments
- Organization
- Engaged Study
- Note Taking
- Textbook Skills
- Test Taking

While each topic was developed individually, please note that the topics are interrelated and recommended practices in one area easily will overlap into another area. Study environments affect engaged study, which affects text book skills, which affects test taking…. Each topic affects and connects with the others. As teachers, we support our students in the development of each of the study skills topics and then assist them in the integration of all into their study skills repertoire. Teachers help their students develop skills for their "toolboxes", moving ever toward the goal of developing independent, metacognitive learners.

REFERENCES

Bucks County Community College. (1997). Cornell note taking and the semantic map citation. Available at http://www.bucks.edu/~specpop/Cornl-ex.htm.

Dodge, J. (1994). *The study skills handbook: More than 75 strategies for better learning.* New York: Scholastic Professional Books.

Keeley, M. (1997). The basics of effective learning: Cornell note taking format. Retrieved December 15, 2010. Available at http://www.bucks.edu/~specpop.Cornl.htm.

McKeachie, W.J. (1988). The need for study strategy training. In C.E. Weinstein, E. T. Goetz, & P. A. Alexander (Eds.), *Learning and study strategies: Issues in assessment, instruction and evaluation* (pp. 3-9). New York: Academic Press.

Pennsylvania Department of Education and Pennsylvania Training and Technical Assistance Network. (2000). *Starting Off Right: Resources for New Teachers.* Harrisburg, PA: Pennsylvania Department of Education.

Robinson, F. P. (1961). *Effective study* (revised ed.). New York: Harper & Brothers, Publishers.

Robinson, S. (1990). *Homework coach: Using your brain to improve learning and grades.* Circle Pines, MN: American Guidance Service.

Simpson, M. L., & Nist, S. L. (1990). Textbook annotation: An effective and efficient study strategy for college students. *Journal of Reading, 34,* 122-129.

Stahl, N., Henk, W., & Georgia State University. (1986). *Tracing the roots of textbook study systems: An extended historical perspective.* College Reading and Learning Assistance Technical Report 86-02. Retrieved from ERIC database.

Wolfe, P. (2001). *Brain matters: Translating research into classroom practice.* Alexandria, VA: Association for Supervision and Curriculum Development.

CHAPTER TEN

Thinking Actively: More Metacognitive Strategies

Kolencik/Hillwig

"In a fluid world, we cannot teach many absolutes about information. It is not the tool that is important; it is the process. If we are to produce lifelong independent learners, then we need to give them the wherewithal to become such—the techniques in addition to the tools, the process, not the product."

Carol Markuson, 1986, p. 10

As you have read, metacognition is students' ability to "predict their performances on various tasks...and to monitor their current levels of mastery and understanding" (National Research Council, 2000, p. 12). With that said, teachers must become more deliberate about not only modeling, but also providing opportunities for metacognitive awareness students need to develop. Teachers need to incorporate effective strategies that empower students to take responsibility for their own learning through self-monitoring and goal setting. Teachers need to provide opportunities for students in the learning environment "to learn to think" and "to think to learn." Teachers should focus on 1) what the student is thinking about content; 2) how the student is thinking about the content; and 3) the student's thinking about his/her own thinking about the content.

When teachers integrate active learning strategies that foster metacognition as a routine part of the learning environment, they can document the many ways that learning has occurred. More importantly, the teacher who effectively fosters metacognition transmits the message that the goal of the classroom is not just to get a good grade, but also to become an independent learner, and that learning to think and thinking to learn is imperative. The authors hope that this section will assist teachers in acquiring a repertoire of metacognitive strategies to integrate into their daily practice.

This chapter contains a plethora of active learning strategies designed to help teachers develop, encourage, and facilitate students' metacognitive skills and to offer them the tools they need for life. The strategies are practical and generic in nature, thus, can be adapted to teach any subject across the curriculum. These strategies enable deeper learning, understanding, and reflection of content and concepts on the part of the student. The strategies discussed in this section ask students to demonstrate their understanding by applying multiple academic skills such as interpreting visual information, conducting an analysis, using criteria, making inferences, and writing coherent explanations. These strategies are designed to encourage students to develop a balanced and dynamic approach to learning, and more importantly, to reflect on how and what they learn or think. The strategies presented range from simple learning, i.e., increasing students' abilities to remember and summarize to relating personally to the curriculum and to each other, to developing students' capacities to reason and use evidence and logic to highlighting students' abilities to imagine, create, and reflect on what they learned and their own learning process (deeper learning). Although one may find that some of the strategies presented will overlap and involve the development of cognitive skills such as predicting, questioning, mapping, or summarizing, all of the strategies presented are metacognitive in nature and involve some form of self-regulation, self-monitoring, or self-evaluation of learning to empower students to become independent in the enterprise of learning and to be better able to manage the learning process.

Effective instructional planning is the lynchpin to using these strategies to find the right "tool" for the right "time." Remember that the overarching goal is the development of students' awareness, understanding, and control of their own learning processes and themselves as learners and individuals. These strategies provide the tools needed to generate a thoughtful classroom and to reflect on one's performance and growth as a learner.

Evidenced-based research indicates that the effective teacher uses a repertoire of strategies to guarantee that each lesson is designed to motivate students' drive toward individuality and originality, in other words, to become independent, lifelong learners. There are a number of learning programs, such as Wiggins and McTighe's Understanding by Design (2005), that provide teachers with helpful information in designing, evaluating, and adjusting units of study so that they lead to deeper learning to meet today's high standards. Wiggins and McTighe (2005) created six facets of understanding as indicators for determining the depth and quality of student comprehension that leads to the development of metacognitive skills. The six components are 1) explanation: summarizing and retelling big ideas and critical concepts; 2) interpretation: making sense of "interpretable" content, such as texts, data, art, and arguments; 3) application: using skills and knowledge in new and authentic contexts; 4) perspective: examining situations from an objective distance and recognizing the legitimacy of different viewpoints; 5) empathy: appreciating and identifying with others' ideas, situations, and motivations, and 6) self-knowledge: developing the self-awareness needed to reflect on one's performance and growth as a learner.

Marzano, Pickering, and Pollock (2001) in *Classroom Instruction That Works: Research-Based Strategies for Increasing Student Achievement* have identified nine distinct classroom practices that make a positive difference in students' performance. These practices attend not only to the product of learning, but also to the process in which students are engaged.

1. identifying similarities and differences
2. summarizing and note taking
3. reinforcing effort and proving recognition
4. homework and practice
5. nonlinguistic representation
6. cooperative learning
7. setting objectives and providing feedback
8. generating and testing hypotheses
9. cues, questions, and advance organizers

The strategies presented in this section reflect best practices about teaching and learning as described earlier by Wiggins and McTighe (2005) and Marzano, Pickering, and Pollock (2001) and specifically address the metacognitive aspects of learning. These distinct classroom practices provide the conceptual framework upon which the authors have divided the strategies. In presenting the strategies, we make reference to three categories that are the phases of instruction:

1) Preparing for learning
2) Presenting content to be learned
3) Integrating and assimilating new knowledge, and assessing and reflecting on learning

In defining these phases, it is not our intent to be prescriptive with regard to the appropriate strategies for each phase of instruction. Rather, we believe that the effective teacher acquires a repertoire of strategies to share with students and selects the appropriate strategy (strategies) in accordance with the enduring understandings, essential questions, content objectives, and performance objectives of the lesson. It is important to provide opportunities for students to "think back" in order to link what they are learning to prior knowledge, test predictions, or forecast outcomes. Above all, a critical aspect is to provide students with the opportunity to reflect on their learning process.

The adage, "There is nothing new under the sun", sets the stage for this section of the text. It is important to see that some of the things that have been in place in classrooms for years are good practices that can be adapted and modified to support current best practices of metacognition. In this segment, the authors will examine the essential elements of instruction that teachers have been using in classrooms for direct instruction. In the 1970s, Madeline Hunter came to the forefront of professional development stating that in order to improve student achievement it was important to improve instruction. The Hunter model included some specific behaviors that teachers were encouraged to use during instruction.

Many of those essential teacher behaviors are readily observed in classrooms around the country on a regular basis. The writing here is not meant to support or refute the work of Hunter, but rather to provide a starting point or framework of classroom instruction that can be used to initiate teaching for metacognition. As the reader works through the following paragraphs, a central theme should be noticed; the teacher facilitates the awareness of metacognitive thinking in students.

When considering the starting point for instruction, teachers have been instructed to use some type of an introductory lesson segment. This introductory set might include a motivator, attention grabber, statement of the objective or accessing prior knowledge. Teachers can consciously impact metacognition simply by the way they formulate a learning objective. When considering that the learning objective states what it is that the student should be able to do at the end of the learning segment, the verb in the objective is the catalyst for metacognition. Words such as *analyze, compare, evaluate, debate, categorize,* and *organize* are examples of verbs that suggest higher level thinking. These verbs represent examples of terminology with which students need to become familiar. Such higher level thinking words should serve as triggers for metacognition. Students need to be accustomed to thinking about how they think in response to what they are being asked to do. It should be typical instructional language for a teacher to state that the students will *analyze* and the students are triggered to think, "When I analyzed something in the past, I had to_____." Calling upon successful past strategies is a critical piece in the metacognitive puzzle.

Activating prior knowledge itself is a metacognitive activity. During this portion of the lesson, students are asked to think about what they already know about a topic or what they had to do in the past to be able to accomplish a task similar to that the teacher is now asking them to do. It might be appropriate for students to complete a K-W-L chart, or participate in a partner or small group discussion where what is already known is called to mind. Another strategy could instruct students to write in their journals indicating the steps that they took in the past when faced with a similar problem or situation. The introductory segment of a lesson sets the stage for metacognition when the teacher plans for instruction with metacognition in mind.

When planning for the lesson development portion of instruction, there are several areas that align with teaching for metacognition. First, teachers have known that modeling is an important instructional practice. Modeling can look like a teacher think aloud where the teacher is actually sharing what his or her thinking processes are, or modeling could be less overt with the teacher providing strategic questioning that models metacognition. The questioning techniques of the teacher during lesson development can actually create the metacognitive thinking environment in the classroom. Planning learning activities where students are required to *create, organize, compare,* or any of the higher order thinking tasks move the student toward metacognition.

Many strategies include a section providing the opportunity for guided practice. If an elementary teacher is providing instruction in the process of long division, students will be afforded guided practice. That same guided practice needs to be considered with metacognition. The manner in which a teacher frames questions and initiates discussion leads to metacognitive development. Let's look a bit closer at that same long division lesson mentioned earlier. Examples of "teacher talk" that enhances metacognition follow:

- "When you were asked to divide previously, what did you need to do?"
- "Do you have anything written in your math notebook that might help you decide how you should go about solving this problem?"
- "Do you think that you will be able to solve this problem mentally, or do you think that you might need to work it out on paper?"
- "Can you think of other ways that you might be able to determine the answer to this problem?"
- "Take some time to think and then tell your partner what you were thinking about."
- "What questions do you still have about long division?"
- "When and where do you believe that you will use long division outside of school?"

The same types of questions can be asked of any student in any content area or grade level. Courses with more complex content lend themselves to more complex questioning, but it is important to remember that these questions can be asked at a level appropriate for young students as well.

All effective lessons include some type of summary and closure. Keep in mind that the teacher doing the summary and closure benefits only the teacher. Research has shown that the individual doing the closure reaps the benefit, thus the students need to be engaged in the closure activity. There are several closure activities that can be utilized, but a few examples are illustrated here:

- "Turn and tell your partner two things that you need to remember from the work you did in class today."
- "Write in your journal one thing that you will remember and one thing that you still need to develop further."
- "If one of your classmates were absent, what important points from today's class would be important to share with him or her?"
- "What surprised you today in our work?"
- "How long do you think it will take you to complete your homework?" "Why do you think that?"

Thinking about the important elements of instructional design provides teachers with a framework for planning the inclusion of metacognitive strategies. The challenge is to be certain that we model metacognition and guide our students toward independently engaging in a metacognitive monologue; where they internalize the self-monitoring and self-reflecting, questioning themselves as they learn.

I. Strategies to prepare for learning

The strategies presented in this section are "bell ringers," that is, anticipatory sets or motivational openers to help engage students' interest at the beginning of the lesson. Think of these strategies as the appetizers of a meal. The first phase, Preparing for Learning, contains opening activities to begin class. The strategies discussed in this section as in all the phases, are designed to encourage students to take an active role in the learning process and to do one or more of the following to promote the metacognitive aspects of learning:

1) Immediate learning involvement: creating initial interest in the content to be studied
2) Instant assessment: learning about students' prior knowledge and attitudes about the content to be studied
3) Team building: Helping students to become acquainted with each other or creating a spirit of cooperation and interdependence

STRATEGY: LEARNING CONTRACTS

Metacognitive Skills: goal setting, reinforcing effort and proving recognition, empathy, perspective, self-knowledge

Strategy Overview and Procedure: A learning contract, also known as learning plan, learning commitment, study plan, learning agreement, or self-development plan, is a collaboratively written agreement between a student and a teacher for the purpose of achieving and attaining specific learning goals, thus, to help students structure their own learning. It can delineate what is to be learned, how it will be learned, and how that learning will be evaluated. The learning contract itself is a written set of varied learning objectives, situations, or outcomes that could encompass items from class attendance or class participation to meeting deadlines. Learning contracts could specify papers to be written, books to be read, projects to be completed, and so forth. Learning contracts can also be used for grading to encourage a student voice in the evaluation process. Students write exactly what is to be accomplished, in what period of time, and, if desired, for what grade or reward. The objectives are clearly specified and outlined, and both the teacher and the student sign the written agreement know as the "contract." The extent to which the teacher is involved in this process is largely dependent upon the grade level and readiness to learn of students as well as where variations arise in the format. The teacher may provide lists of objectives, activities, and assignments from which students choose, thus, the teacher is taking a more active hand in the process. Depending on the grade level, a teacher may prefer to take a more hands-off approach, allowing the student to define almost the entire contract. Learning contracts allow students to make important choices about what, how, and when to learn, thereby facilitating the development of a partnership learning environment in which students are likely to retain more information, make better use of information, and be more highly motivated to learn than in teacher-directed learning environments.

Learning contracts have several advantages. First, they encourage students to be self-directing and self-monitoring, two critical metacognitive skills. Second, the commitment to keep the contact may motivate students. Learning contracts challenge learners to tap into the intrinsic motivators (Knowles, 1986). Third, the learning contract can be individualized to meet the needs of each student. Fourth, the mere process of drafting of the learning contract, ingeniously challenges students to think through why they are undertaking to learn something.

In sum, contracts provide a way to deal with the wide differences among any group of learners, increase student motivation for learning, facilitate the development of mutual respect between the student and the teacher, provide for more individualized mode of instruction, and foster the metacognitive skills of self-directedness and self-monitoring which may increase self-esteem, responsibility, creativity, and self-fulfillment. The use of learning contracts allows students to structure their own learning to be an active participant in the process of education.

Keep in mind that education has to be an *active* rather than *passive* process. To be active, students must participate in the process of education and become more independent and responsible for their own learning. Learning contacts are an excellent strategy to do that. According to Frymier (1965), "Allowing students to decide which grade they wish to strive for, which activities they will engage in, and how they will demonstrate that they have satisfactorily completed their studies permits a teacher to seize upon powerful motivating forces within individual students. ... This notion shifts responsibility for learning from the teacher to the student, but at the same time offers an incentive by insuring success under known conditions. Students are challenged without being threatened" (pp. 263, 264).

Although there are many different ways to design a learning contract by incorporating as many or as few elements as one wishes, there is a general format which the majority of learning contracts follow:

1. Identify what content will be learned
2. Specify the methods and strategies that will be used to learn the content
3. Specify resources to be used in order to learn the content
4. Specify the type of evidence that will be used to demonstrate learning
5. Specify how the evidence will be validated, and by whom

A sample template appears in Table 10.1.

Learning Contract				
What are you going to learn? (objectives; knowledge, skills, attitude, values)	How are you going to learn it? (resources/ strategies)	Target date for completion	How are you going to know that you learned it? (evidence/ metacognition)	How are you going to prove you learned? (verification of learning)

Table 10.1 Learning Contract

Contracting can also be used as a means to manage inappropriate student behavior in the classroom. Table 10.2 illustrates a self-monitoring behavior contact.

Self-Monitoring Behavior Contract
1. The responsibility I still need to develop is 2. The specific behavior that I was displaying was 3. This behavior is affecting my learning because 4. This behavior is affecting others around me because 5. My personal plan to improve my behavior and develop the above responsibility is My signature proves that I have reflected on my inappropriate behavior. I am willing to work with my teacher to meet ALL my responsibilities. Student Signature_____ Guardian Signature _____ Date _____.

Table 10.2 Self-Monitoring Behavior Contract

STRATEGY: ANTICIPATION GUIDE

Metacognitive Skills: activate and use prior knowledge; prediction

Strategy Overview and Procedure: Similar to a K-W-L strategy, the anticipation guide, also known as a reaction guide or prediction guide, is an active pre-reading strategy. The anticipation guide prepares students by asking them to react in writing to a series of essential questions/statements related to the content material before reading. This strategy not only helps students activate their prior knowledge about a topic, but also enables students to clarify their ideas and opinions about a topic by completing a guide. This strategy is also a helpful technique for eliciting students' misconceptions about a subject. Additionally, the guide enables students to focus their attention on the major points during their reading and to provide a framework for discussing the text after their reading. Students become actively involved in the dynamics of reading a specified selection because they have an opportunity to talk about the topic before reading about it.

The purpose is threefold: 1) to make critical connections to prior knowledge and experiences before reading; 2) to provide reinforcement of key concepts after reading as well as challenges their prior knowledge; and 3) to stimulate students' interest in the topic or content. Anticipation guides work best with material that prompts students to form an opinion.

One of the greatest benefits of the Anticipation Guide is that it offers teachers the opportunity to witness metacognitive growth. Teachers are able to determine the stages of students' thinking. For example, teachers can see where students are in their thinking in the pre-reading stage and then they get to listen in on students' new learning, as reflected in discussions, during the post-reading stage. In sum, anticipation guides open new avenues of learning for students. Completing an anticipation guide provides students with an opportunity to make critical connections about the new topics and the new vocabulary they are studying and what they already know about the content.

To develop an anticipation guide, follow these steps:

1. Identify several major concepts related to the reading assignment that students are expected to learn.
2. Using the template in Table 10.3 develop a list of three to five concise statements. Do not use questions. Statements should be precise and not be abstract or generalizations. Statements may reflect common misconceptions about the subject or indicative of students' prior knowledge.

3. Students respond to each statement before reading and defend their beliefs and opinions.
4. Openly discuss student responses/predictions as a class prior to reading. Note any recurring themes in the discussion. Also, note any opposing or contradictory points of view.
5. Instruct students to read the assignment. Instruct students to make comments on their written answer sheet, noting agreement and disagreement between their answers and the author's message or purpose.
6. Students respond to each statement after reading and explain why their before and after answers are different.
7. Students engage in a summarizing discussion, expressing how the reading selection reinforced or challenged their prior knowledge.

Anticipation guide				
Directions: Respond to each statement before reading. Respond to each statement after reading.				
Pre-reading		Statement	Post-reading	
Agree	Disagree		Agree	Disagree

Table 10.3 Anticipation Guide

STRATEGY: TRADING PLACES

Metacognitive Skills: self-monitoring, self-regulation, problem solving

Strategy Overview and Procedure: This strategy allows students to exchange options and consider new ideas, values, or solutions to problems. It's a great way to promote self-disclosure or an active exchange of viewpoints. To implement this strategy, begin by giving students one or more sticky notes. Decide whether the activity will work better by limiting the students to one contribution or several. Ask students to write on their note(s) one of the following: a) a value they hold; b) an experience they have had recently; c) a creative idea or solution to a problem you've posed; d) a question they have about the subject matter you are studying; e) an opinion they hold about the topic of study; f) a fact about themselves or the topic of study. Ask students to stick the note(s) on their clothing and circulate around the room reading each other's notes. Next, have students mingle once again and negotiate a trade of notes with one another. The trade should be based on a desire to possess a particular value, experience, ideas, question, option, or fact for a short period of time. Set the rule that all trades have to be two-way. Encourage students to make as many trades as they like. Finally, reconvene the class and ask students to share what trades they made and why. For example, "I traded for a note that David had, stating that he has traveled to England. I would really like to travel there because I want to see Buckingham Palace." A variation of this strategy is to ask students to form subgroups rather than trade notes, and have them discuss the contents of their notes.

STRATEGY: RECONNECT AND REFLECT

Metacognitive Skill: self-reflection

Strategy Overview and Procedure: In any class that meets over time, it is sometimes helpful to spend a few minutes at the beginning of class reconnecting with students. Explain that you think it is valuable to spend a few minutes reconnecting before proceeding with the day's lesson. Pose one or more of the following questions to the students:

- What do you remember about our last class? What stands out for you?
- Have you read/thought out/done something that was stimulated by our last class?
- What interesting experiences have you had between classes
- What's on your mind right now (e.g., a worry) that might interfere with your ability to give full attention to today's class?
- How do you feel today?

Obtain responses using learning partners, small group discussion, or open class discussion or by having students write in their journal. A variation of this strategy is to present two questions, concepts, or pieces of information covered in the previous class. Ask students to vote for the one they would most like you to review with the class.

STRATEGY: TICKET IN THE DOOR

Metacognitive Skills: self-assessment, self-reflection, transfer

Strategy Overview and Procedure: As each student enters the room, have him or her tell the teacher one item s/he recalls from yesterday's lesson. A variation to this admission ticket is for the teacher to write a question or prompt on the board and have students respond while they wait for class to begin. For example, the teacher could pose a question about today's content or have students reflect on yesterday's lesson with such questions as 1) What did you learn in yesterday's lesson that was new to you? or 2) What questions did you have about yesterday's lesson? The teacher can then use this question/prompt as a springboard to begin the lesson. Instead of a teacher-generated question, students can be asked to write a review question about yesterday's content, or pose a question about the topic being studied, or a point of confusion.

Several other miscellaneous bell ringers that trigger metacognitive skills are:

- Show students objects or pictures related to the content to help students activate background and prior knowledge
- Blend content with each student's interest and daily life
- Connect content with current event and students' daily lives
- Open with quote; story, poem. song, cartoon
- KWL chart : What do I know; what do I wonder; what did I learn
- KWLH chart: What do I know; what I want to learn; what I learn as I read; how I can learn more
- KWS chart: what I know; what I want to learn; what are the possible sources

II. Strategies for the Presentation of Content to Be Learned

The strategies presented in this section are declarative in nature and center around students acquiring knowledge, skills, and dispositions These strategies are what we call the "learn to think." These techniques or strategies can be compared to the entrée of a meal. Remember that although the content may be determined by national or state standards and the curricula or texts adopted by a school district, it is the teacher-determined learning strategies in which the students engage that will determine the level of learning achieved. This section contains strategies that can be used when one is at the heart of the lesson. The strategies are designed to enhance a teacher-led instruction and push students to think, feel, and apply what they are learning.

Keep in mind that class discussion plays a critical role in the metacognitive learning process during the presentation of the content to be learned. Hearing a wide variety of views and sharing opinions and perspectives challenges students' thinking. The teacher's role during a group discussion is to facilitate the flow of comments from students. Although it is not necessary to interject after each student speaks, periodically assisting the group with their contributions complements the teaching and learning process. The following points are offered to the teacher to facilitate discussion that promotes "learning to think."

1) Paraphrase what a student has said so that the student feels understood and the other students can hear a concise summary of what's been said at greater length. For example, "So, what you're saying is that you have to be very careful about the words you use because a particular person might be offended by them." Other members of the class can be asked to restate in his or her own words what the classmate just said.

2) Check for understanding against the words of a student or ask a student to clarify what he or she is saying. For example, "Are you saying that this political correctness has gone too far? I'm not sure that I understand exactly what you meant. Could you please run it by us again?"

3) Compliment a novel idea or insightful comment. For example, "That's a good point. I'm glad that you brought that to our attention."

4) Elaborate on a student's contribution to the discussion with examples, or pose questions to examine the problem, concept, or issue from an alternate perspective. For example, "Your comments provide an interesting point from the minority perspective. We could also consider how the majority would view the same situation."

5) Energize a discussion by picking up the pace, interjecting humor, or, if necessary, prodding the group to think out of the box. For example, "We have a lot of quiet people in this class! Here's a challenge for you. For the next two minutes, let's see how many words you can think of that are no longer politically correct."

6) Disagree gently with a student's comments to stimulate further discussion. For example, "I can see where you are coming from, but I'm not sure that what you are describing is always the case. Has anyone else had an experience that is different than Frank's experience?"

7) Mediate differences of opinion between students and relieve any tension that may be brewing. For example, "I think that Joan and Ashley are not really disagreeing with each other, but are just bringing out two different sides of this issue."

8) Pull together ideas by showing their relationship to each other. For example, "As you can see from Juan's and Margaret's comments, the words we use can offend people. Both of them have given us an example of how they feel excluded by gender-bound words."

9) Change the group process by altering the method for obtaining participation or moving the group to a stage of evaluating ideas that have been placed before the group. For example, "Let's break into smaller groups and see if you can come up with some criteria for establishing what constitutes bullying."

10) Summarize and record, if desired, the major views of the group. For example, "I have noted three major ideas that have come from the group's discussion as to when words are harmful: 1) they exclude some people; 2) they insult some people; and 3) they are determined only by the majority culture."

11) Conclude the discussion by discussing students' affect. Invite students to process their feelings that the activity elicited and share the insights and learning it contained by posing questions. For example, "What feelings do you have about this experience?" "Why do you feel this way?" "What is it that you are most worried about?" "What skills or knowledge do you feel you need to have?"

Keep in mind that learning partners or "study buddies" (two students working together) is another viable alternative to an open class discussion or a small group discussion. Having students work on tasks or discuss key questions with the student seated next to them involves everybody but doesn't require as much time. It's hard to get left out in a pair and it's also hard to hide in one. A pair is good group configuration for developing a supportive relationship and/or for working on complex activities that would not lend themselves to a large-group configuration. Learning partners can be short or long term. A learning partnership can undertake a wide variety of quick tasks or more time-consuming assignments much easier than a group. The following list provides suggestions for the use of learning partners:

1) Discuss a short written document together

2) Interview each other concerning partner's reactions to an assigned reading, a lecture, or a video

3) Critique or edit each other's written work

4) Question your partner about an assigned reading

5) Recap a lesson or class session together

6) Develop questions together to ask the teacher or pose to the class

7) Analyze a case problem, exercise, or experiment together

8) Test each other

9) Respond to a question posed by the teacher

10) Compare notes taken in class

STRATEGY: TRANSFER JOURNAL

Metacognitive Skills: self-monitoring, application, transfer, reflection

Strategy Overview and Procedure: Teachers sometimes think that students will automatically take what has been learned in one class and apply or transfer it to other classes, places, or areas. Unfortunately, students often do not make that connection. A transfer journal plays a critical role in the metacognitive process by helping students make those connections. The transfer journal contains three categories, the big idea, the interpretation of the idea, and the application of the idea. The application forces students to make connections to other subjects and think about their insights from the idea. Table 10.4 provides a template for a transfer journal.

Transfer Journal				
Idea	Interpretation	Application/ Connection	Application/ Transfer	Application Insights/ Reflection
What is the Big Idea? (copy phrases/ sentences exactly from text)	What does it mean? (write in your words)	How can you connect the idea to another subject?	How can you apply or transfer the idea to your life?	What insight or reflection do you have from the idea?

Table 10.4 Transfer Journal

STRATEGY: PROCESS WRITING

Metacognitive Skills: self-assessment, self-regulation, self-refection, transfer

Strategy Overview and Procedure: Process writing, which is nothing more than a reading-writing task, is one of the best cognitively demanding strategies that can be used in the classroom. Process writing when used in conjunction with texts that students read, clarifies students' thinking and provides a fine opportunity for students to develop numerous metacognitive skills. This writing-to-learn strategy not only requires students to select and organize content, it required them to make content connections from their reading as they compose their own new texts. Using process logs highly promotes the use of metacognitive strategies, specifically, self-assessment. Additionally, process logs are not only effective for developing time management and organizational skills, but also for building problem-solving and creative thinking skills. Writing assignments allow teachers to easily check for understanding of content and ideas. The procedure is simple. Ask students to read the assigned article, story, chapter, etc. After completing the reading assignment, ask students to respond to the following prompts: (note: select the prompts that are appropriate for the reading assignment)

1. Explain the new information or process (content concepts, ideas, etc.) in your own words.
2. Explain how the new information fits in with something you already know.
3. How does the new information cause you to change your mind about something you thought you knew?
4. Explain the newly learned process to a friend in class.
5. Describe how you can use the new information that you have learned.
6. Explain why it is important to learn this information.
7. Explain those parts of the process or information that you consider to be difficult for others to understand.
8. Explain the tools, equipment, materials, and/or safety procedures to be followed when conducting the process or procedure.
9. Explain areas of the process or procedure where errors could be made which would affect the end result.
10. Describe how you would explain this process to a new employee at your workplace.

STRATEGY: PARAGRAPH SHRINKING

Metacognitive Skills: summarization, activation of students' background knowledge

Strategy Overview and Procedure: Students read in pairs with one reading a section of the text and the other summarizing. Roles are then reversed.

STRATEGY: JIGSAW

Metacognitive Skills: assimilation, self-monitoring

Strategy Overview and Procedure: Divide students into groups of four, five, or six. Divide the material to be learned into four, five, or six sections. Assign each team member to one of the subsection of material. S/he should work on that material and how it will be learned. Each of these subgroups is known as an "expert" group. After students have mastered the material in their expert group, they each return to their original groups. Each expert then teaches the information s/he has learned to the other members of the group.

STRATEGY: THREE'S A CHARM

Metacognitive Skill: summarization

Strategy Overview and Procedure: After the presentation of a teacher-directed lesson, divide the class into teams of four or six. Have each member of a team choose another member to be a partner. During the first step, have individuals interview their partners by asking clarifying and probing questions. During the second step, have partners reverse the roles. In the final step, have members share their partner's response with the team. An additional step can be added to this strategy by asking students to individually write a summary statement about the new knowledge they gleaned from the discussion.

STRATEGY: THREE-MINUTE REVIEW

Metacognitive Skills: summarization, self-reflection, self-assessment

Strategy Overview and Procedure: Prior to beginning a lecture or discussion, divide the class into teams. Stop and give teams three minutes to review what's been said and ask clarifying questions. Invite each team to arrive at a summary statement (a main idea) of what was presented. Write the responses on the board. Take time to discuss any differences among teams. At the end of the lesson, invite teams to review the summary statements and to arrive at the most appropriate ones for the section of the lesson or the entire lesson. Additionally, at the end of the lesson, have each team of students create a graphic organizer from the responses.

STRATEGY: QUICKWRITE

Metacognitive Skills: activate background and prior knowledge, transfer, reflection

Strategy Overview and Procedure: The quickwrite, which is similar to freewriting, is a writing strategy developed by Elbow (1998) whose purpose is to emphasis content rather than mechanics. The quickwrite enables students to explain in writing their understanding of the content being studied. The purpose of the quickwrite is to provide an opportunity for each student to focus, think, recall prior knowledge, and formulate ideas in writing in a limited amount of time. A quickwrite can be done at any time during the lesson and enables students to react to the new information by responding in writing. Quickwrites engage students in focused and fluent thinking that becomes transferred onto paper through writing. Students are given several minutes of quiet time to think and write simultaneously. The quickwrite requires an open-ended writing prompt about the content that students can respond to in writing in two or three minutes. Since the time is limited, the prompt should be simple and concise and not complex in order for students to focus clearly and quickly about the concept. An example of a quickwrite prompt to activate background and prior knowledge might be "why should people follow rules and laws?" Another example of a quickwrite prompt might be to ask what are the similarities (or differences) between ancient and modern Greece.

STRATEGY: QUESTIONING THE AUTHOR (QTA)

Metacognitive Skills: prediction, self-monitoring, activation of prior knowledge

Strategy Overview and Procedure: Questioning the Author (QtA) is an active reading pedagogical strategy that employs the question to increase student engagement with text at varying levels. Beck, McKeown, Sandora, Kucan, and Worthy (1996) developed Questioning the Author (QtA) to help students become actively involved in reading text during the reading process. This strategy differs significantly from other active engagement strategies that concentrate on interaction with text after it is read. QtA focuses on having "students grapple with and reflect on what an author is trying to say in order to build a representation from it" (p. 387). While students are reading, teachers pose Queries, which are designed to support and encourage students as they deal with texts. The Queries are designed to invite "understanding, interpretation, and elaboration by having students explore the meaning of what is written in the texts they read" (p. 387).

The Question the Author strategy has three main components: planning the implementation, creating queries, and developing discussions. The following steps can be used as a guide to effectively use QtA:

1. Before using the strategy, prepare students by informing them that they will be learning a new way of reading and dealing with text. The teacher should make it clear to students that the any author can potentially be fallible. Letting students know that the content presented is someone's ideas, a person that can sometimes makes mistakes, will

provide students the opportunity to understand they have the right to question the author.

2. Model for students parts of QtA by first selecting a piece of text and then demonstrating the kinds of thoughts and considerations a reader should make when reading. Require students to follow along using a copy of the text either on the overhead projector or document camera. If warranted, the teacher may want to provide students their own individual copy. The teacher should read aloud, stop at difficult or interesting parts, and think aloud about anything that is confusing . The teacher should ensure that they are saying aloud when the author's writing is confusing or not clearly written. This would be a perfect opportunity for students to share their own experience with text. Ask students the following questions: What did you find confusing while reading? How would you write or communicate that part differently? What do you think the author is trying to say? What was written clearly and succinctly? This modeling of the think aloud and discussion is an important step and should be modeled several times if necessary. It is also important to inform students that they will be responsible for this type of interaction and engagement with text This modeling process is a critical step in developing metacognitive skills.

3. Planning for QtA involves three considerations (Beck et al., 1997): identifying the major understandings students should construct and anticipate potential problems in the text, segment the text to focus on information needed to build understanding, and develop queries that promote understanding. First, the teacher critically reads the texts and identifies any major concepts that students much construct from the text while anticipating any problems that readers may encounter. The teacher should consider this exercise a conversation with the author; a chance to get to the root of all understanding and problems with the text. "Teachers who find themselves doing extra work when they read can be reasonably sure that their students also will encounter difficulties and may not be able to resolve the problems without support" (Beck et al., 1997, p. 51).

4. The teacher must segment the text by determining where to stop reading in order to initiate the query that will develop into a discussion. It is important to note that the text should be segmented where understanding should occur or where confusion may occur. It is not necessary to stop at the end of paragraphs or sections.

5. The teacher must then create and develop queries. Queries are a vital part of the QtA process and differ significantly from questions. Questions are usually used to assess students' comprehension of text, evaluate individual student responses, prompt teacher-to-student interactions, and used before or after reading. Queries, on the other hand, assist students in grappling with text ideas to construct meaning, facilitate group discussions, and are used during initial reading (Beck et al., 1997). Questions have traditionally been teacher-initiated while queries serve as the focal point of the lesson or interaction with text. Queries allow the teacher to be a facilitator of the discussion in the library or classroom. There are three types of queries to be used during the reading: initiating, follow-up, and narrative. Initiating queries include What is the author trying to say? What is the author's message? What is the author talking about?

The second type of query, follow-up, helps students look at "what the text *means* rather than what the text *says*" (Beck et al., 1997, p. 37). Examples of follow-up prompts include What does the author mean? Does the author explain this clearly? Does this make sense with knowing what the author told us previously? Why do you think the author tells us this now?

Finally, the third type of query is used specifically with narrative text. These queries differ significantly from the queries used with expository text since the structure and nature of text differs in a story. Queries used for narrative text may deal with story structure, characters, and/or plot development. Examples of such queries may include: How do things look for this character now? How has the author let you know that something has changed? Does that change make sense given what we know about the character(s)?

The teacher can use the Query Tally Sheet in Table 10.5 to document the types of queries asked while interacting with a text. This method will ensure that the queries are more extended discussion oriented and less recall oriented. Development of discussion is an important element of QtA. It is the job of the students to construct meaning from the text. The teacher should spend little time explaining text to students. Instead students should be grappling with the text and dealing with the uncertainty themselves with guidance from the teacher. Finally, the teacher should repeat the queries for each segment or section of text.

Query Tally Sheet	
Date: _____	Text: _____
Name of Student	Number of questions for answered correctly
Ex: Jim Jones	5/6

Table 10.5 Query Tally Sheet

III. Integration/Assimilation of New Knowledge/Reflection

The strategies presented in this section involve the "learning forever" process. They represent the think to learn progression. Metaphorically, these strategies are the dessert part of the meal.

STRATEGY: TICKET TO LEAVE

Metacognitive Skills: self-assessment, self-monitoring, and reflection

Strategy Overview and Procedure: This strategy gives students the opportunity to summarize what they have learned and to present their summary to others. It is an excellent strategy for students to examine, recap, and reflect on what they have learned during the class period.

1. Explain to students that providing a summary of what they learned in class and this type of self-reflection promotes self-assessment and deeper learning.

2. Students are given one minute to respond in writing to a specific question, such as:

    "What was the most meaningful thing you learned from today's lesson?"

    "What did you learn about the content you studied today?"

    "What are the major topics we have examined?"

    "What experiences have you had today?"

    "How will you use or apply the information you learned today in the future?"

    "What questions do you still have?"

    "What didn't you understand?"

    "What do you now believe?"

    "What new skills did you learn?"

    "What do I need to improve?"

    "What ideas or suggestions are you taking away from this class?"

3. After students have composed their written response, divide students into groups of two to four members.

4. Ask each group to create their own summary of the class session.

5. Encourage them to create an outline, a mind map, a drawing, or a musical rap, that will enable them to communicate the summary to others. To vary this strategy, ask students to summarize the topic by creating an acronym. Have students brainstorm everything can remember about the topic studied and then elaborate on those ideas to create a phrase that starts with each letter in the topic.

6. Invite groups to share their summaries verbally.

STRATEGY: 3-2-1 COUNTDOWN OF LEARNING

Metacognitive Skills: self-assessment, self-monitoring, and reflection

Strategy Overview and Procedure: The 3-2-1 countdown of learning is used at the end of the class to summarize a particular topic. Students are asked to respond to the following: three most important things learned, two questions that still need to be answered, and one way their learning connects to what they knew before.

STRATEGY: ONE-MINUTE EXIT SLIPS

Metacognitive Skills: goal-setting, self-assessment, self-monitoring, summarization, reflection

Strategy Overview and Procedure: At the end of class, have students construct a question related to the topic studied and to set a learning goal for the next day. Additionally, students write a one-minute paper summarizing what they learned from the lesson and how they can apply that learning.

STRATEGY: TEXTBOOK ACTIVITY GUIDE

Metacognitive Skills: self-monitoring

Strategy Overview and Procedure: Davey's (1986) textbook activity guide (TAG) is an excellent metacognitive strategy for use in the classroom because it is based on self-monitoring components. The textbook activity guide, which requires students to work in pairs, is a set of strategy codes directing students to complete one activity for each text portion read. For example, students may make predictions about a textbook passage, discuss the text with their partner, retell or write a response to the information, or draw a concept map or web. The activity guide also includes self-monitoring codes that allow students to indicate which portion of the text passage needs further clarification. Textbook activity guides enable students to monitor their comprehension by indicating the degree to which they understand a particular question or segment of text. Textbook activity guides may vary in length depending on the content to be learned. The first time this guide is introduced to students, it is critical that the teacher model, explain, and demonstrate the use of the textbook activity guide before assigning students to work in pairs. Additionally, it is critical for the teacher to stress the purpose for using this type of guide. It is important for students to understand the textbook activity guide's value as a self-monitoring strategy to enhance deeper learning. As students become proficient in the use of these guides, students should be able to construct their own guides, depending upon the grade level.

The strategy codes are:
- RR=read and retell in your own words
- DP=read and discuss with partner
- PP=predict with partner
- WR=Write a response on your own
- SK=skim; read quickly for purpose stated and discuss with partner
- GO MOC =organize information in, map, outline, or chart, i.e., some type of graphic organizer

The self-monitoring codes are:
- Checkmark=I understand this information
- Question mark=I'm not sure if I understand
- X=I do not understand and I need to review

Strategy codes are explained at the topic of the activity guide and placed beside each question to cue the desired type of response and are placed beside each question to cue the desired type of response. The teacher can change or add strategy codes as needed for a given lesson. Developing a textbook activity guide is a five-step process. First, the teacher must clearly identify the lesson objective(s). The teacher must clarify what students should know and be able to do by the end of the lesson. Second, review the text and pick out the hearings, portions, and diagrams that consistently relate to the objective(s). Third, select text features to be used in the activity guide and sequences the features appropriately. Fourth, match the reading/study task to the objective. This is where the strategy codes are used. When the objective calls for making an inference or brainstorming of prior knowledge, the most appropriate task might be to discuss the selection with a partner. If the teacher wants students to sequence, organize, or show relationships, a logical choice would be to have students make a map, chart, outline or some type of graphic organizer. Choose one task for each text portion of the guide. Fifth, create a self-monitoring system that is easily understood by students. Use self-monitoring prompts such as, "I understand", "I'm not sure if I understand", and "I do not understand and I need more help." Doing this enables the teacher to simply walk around the classroom to eavesdrop, check for understanding, and determine which areas may require additional review or explanation. Table 10. 6 Textbook Activity Guide shows an example of the textbook activity guide.

Textbook Activity Guide

Name _____

Topic:_____

STRATEGY CODES:
- RR = read and retell in your own words
- DP = read and discuss with partner
- PP = predict with partner
- WR = write a response on your own
- SK = skim; read quickly for purpose stated and discuss with partner
- GOMOC = organize information in a graphic organizer, map, outline, or chart

SELF-MONITORING CODES
- ____ I understand this information
- ____ I'm not sure if I understand
- ____ I do not understand and I need more help

1. ____ PP pp.100-107. Survey the title, headings, pictures, and charts. What do you expect to learn from this section?

2. ____ WR As you are reading, jot down three or more new words and definitions for your vocabulary collection.

3. ____ RR pp. 100-101, first three paragraphs

4. ____ DP pp. 102-103, next three paragraphs
   a. teacher-constructed content question
   b. teacher-constructed content question

5. ____ GOMOC pp. 104-110
   Make an outline of the information.
   I. _____   II. _____   III. _____
   A.   A.   A.
   B.   B.   B.
   C.   C.   C.

6. ____ SK p. 111 first four paragraphs
   Paraphrase the key idea

7. ____ DP pp. 112-115
   teacher-constructed content question

8. ____ WR p. 116 next to last paragraph
   Define the word....Jot down three other words that a similar in meaning

9. ____ WR summarize what you've learned

10. ____ WR the most important concept I learned was

Table 10. 6 Textbook Activity Guide

STRATEGY: WRAP IT UP

Metacognitive Skills: self-assessment, self-monitoring, reflection

Strategy Overview and Procedure: The wrap it up is an effective oral reflective technique that teachers can use in the middle of or at the end of a lesson to find out how students feel and what they remember about a lesson. The teacher writes a few prompts on the board. Prompts should be insightful and reflective in nature. Some sample wrap it up prompts are:

- One thing I learned is...
- The thing that really surprised me is...
- One thing I'll remember 5 years from now is...
- If I had taught this lesson, I would have...

The class is divided so that each student knows which prompt s/he will answer. Provide sufficient wait time to allow everyone to reflect. Go around the room and call on each student to complete the prompt assigned. If time permits, follow with discussion.

STRATEGY: STOP AND SWITCH

Metacognitive Skills: summarization, synthesis, self-reflection

Strategy Overview and Procedure: This metacognitive summary strategy is an effective method to bring closure to a lesson. Begin by asking students to write down five things they have learned. Give students two minutes to complete this task. Second, ask them to pair with a partner. Third, using a watch to time the activity, tell one person to talk for two minutes about what s/he has learned. Fourth, at the end of **two minutes**, call for a Stop/Switch. The other student talks for two minutes, but is not permitted to repeat anything that has been stated by his/her partner. Fifth, when time is up, call for a Stop/Switch. Begin the cycle again, alternating partners and not repeating anything that was said for one minute. Sixth, at the end of the two one minute intervals, call for a Stop/Switch, and ask each pair thirty seconds to write **one sentence** that summarizes the key idea of what they have learned. Share the findings as a whole class.

STRATEGY: PMI=PLUS, MINUS, INTERESTING

Metacognitive Skills: decision-making, summarization

Strategy Overview and Procedure: This strategy, created more than two decades ago by DeBono (1985) stands for pluses, minuses, and interesting. This decision-making strategy is first done on an individual basis. Ask students

THINKING ACTIVELY: MORE METACOGNITIVE STRATEGIES | 171

to make a PMI chart (see Table 10.7 PMI template). After students make the chart, give them a statement to consider. The statement should reflect the content that is being studied at the time. Additionally, the statement should require students to apply, analyze, synthesize, and evaluate that knowledge in order to complete each column in the chart. The statement should present something with more than one side, and it can be phrased either positively or negatively. The following are examples of sample statements: 1) Capital punishment is a deterrent to crime, 2) Global warming is a myth, 3) Recycling costs more money to do that it is worth. First, students individually record the positive, negative, and other interesting aspects in regard to the statement. After students finish, ask them to share their responses with a partner or small group. During this process, encourage students to revise their chart in light of what they have discussed with their classmates. Aspects are shared in a whole group setting. A large version of the chart can be created on the board and individual students or groups can be asked to post their strongest plus, minus, and interesting point. When all the responses have been listed, group discussion occurs where students consider all alternatives and reflect on where the strongest points lie. Usually, one column has the majority of responses, and these points are often the most compelling to support the statement. Finally, ask students to reexamine their initial positions and individually record the strongest plus and minus point that support the statement from their viewpoint. This strategy enables students to discuss how they feel about a topic. It can also be used a summarization strategy to recapitulate the lesson of the day's content.

PMI Chart Template		
Statement:		
Pluses	Minuses	Interesting

Table 10.7 PMI Template

REFERENCES

Beck, I. L. et al. (1997). *Questioning the author: An approach for enhancing student engagement with text.* Newark, DE: International Reading Association, 1997.

Davey, B. (1986). Using textbook activity guides to help student learn from textbooks. *Journal of Reading, 29,* 489-494.

DeBono, E. (1985). *Six thinking hats* (rev. ed.). Boston: Little, Brown.

Elbow, P. (1998). *Writing without teachers.* New York: Oxford University Press.

Frymier, J. R. (1965). *The nature of educational method.* Columbus, OH: Charles E. Merrill.

Knowles, M. S. (1986). *Using learning contracts.* San Francisco: Jossey-Bass.

Marzano, R. J., Pickering, D. J., & Pollock, J. E. (2001). *Classroom instruction that works: Research-based strategies for increasing student achievement.* Alexandria, VA: ASCD.

Markuson, C. (1986). "Making it happen, taking charge of the information curriculum." *School Library Media Quarterly, 15,* 37-40.

National Research Council. (2000). *How people learn: Brain, mind experience, and school.* J. D. Bransford, A. L. Brown, & R. R. Cocking (Eds.). Commission on Behavioral and Social Sciences and Education. Washington, DC: National Academy Press.

Wiggins, G., & McTighe, J. (2005). *Understanding by design.* Alexandria, VA: Association for Supervision and Curriculum Development.

SECTION FOUR

Appendices

Thinking as a Learner: Best Practices

Pressley and Hilden (2006) suggest the following best practice strategies teachers can incorporate into their daily routine to help students use metacognitive strategies:

1. Remember that multiple strategies are a key aspect of solving problems. Monitor students' knowledge and awareness of strategies for effective learning outcomes.
2. Model effective strategies for students.
3. Give students many opportunities to practice the strategies. Provide guidance, support, and feedback throughout the process.
4. Encourage students to monitor the effectiveness of their new strategies in comparison to the effectiveness of old strategies.
5. Always remember it takes students a considerable amount of time to learn how to use an effective strategy. Be patient and provide encouragement.
6. Motivation is key to use the strategies. Encourage students to set goals for learning effective strategies.
7. When planning lessons, always plan to ask questions to guide students' thinking. For example, "How can proofreading help me in writing a paper?"; "Why is it important periodically to stop when I'm reading and try to understand what is being said so far?"; or "What is the purpose of learning this information?"

Pressley, M., & Hilden, K. (2006). Cognitive strategies. In W. Damon & R. Lerner (Eds.), *Handbook of child psychology* (6th ed., pp. 512-574). New York: Wiley.

Thinking as a Learner: Self-monitoring Checkbric

Questions to help students develop metacognitively and reflect on their learning.

1. What did I think about when we were learning about ...
2. What did I think about when I was completing this assignment?
3. Why is this important?
4. What are two strengths of my work?
5. What strategies supported my learning?
6. What part was most difficult for me?
7. What would I do differently?
8. How could I improve?
9. How organized and effective have I been in completing this project?
10. What have I done to help me understand or learn about this topic?
11. Did I manage my time well?
12. How does this connect to what I already know?
13. What do I still wonder about?
14. What are two questions I still have?
15. How has my thinking changed?
16. Could I easily summarize what I've learned and tell someone briefly about my learning?
17. What is the one thing I will remember?
18. How can I use this information in my life?
19. What new goal can I set because of my work?
20. How do I feel as a learner?

Thinking as a Learner: Metacognitive Rubric

Metacognitive Skill	I Do This Infrequently	I Do This Inconsistently	I Do This Frequently	I Do This Always
I am aware of effective and ineffective thinking strategies and use the necessary strategy to obtain the outcome I desire.				
I periodically monitor the thinking strategies I use.				
I use good strategies for forming concepts.				
I construct my own thinking rather than just passively accept what others think.				
I use a system for solving problems.				
When solving problems, I use strategies such as goal setting and working backward in time.				
I don't fall into problem-solving traps such as daydreaming, lack of motivation, or not controlling my emotions.				
When solving problems, I set criteria for my success and evaluate how well I have met my problem-solving goals.				
I make a practice of rethinking and redefining problems over an extended period of time.				
I am good at creative thinking.				
I develop my ability to apply my prior knowledge to new problems and situations.				
I evaluate my methods and materials.				
I develop a commitment to personal achievement and to do quality work.				

INDEX

Educational PSYCHOLOGY

Critical Pedagogical Perspectives

Greg S. Goodman, *General Editor*

Educational Psychology: Critical Pedagogical Perspectives is a series of relevant and dynamic works by scholars and practitioners of critical pedagogy, critical constructivism, and educational psychology. Reflecting a multitude of social, political, and intellectual developments prompted by the mentor Paulo Freire, books in the series enliven the educator's process with theory and practice that promote personal agency, social justice, and academic achievement. Often countering the dominant discourse with provocative and yet practical alternatives, *Educational Psychology: Critical Pedagogical Perspectives* speaks to educators on the forefront of social change and those who champion social justice.

For further information about the series and submitting manuscripts, please contact:

> Dr. Greg S. Goodman
> Department of Education
> Clarion University
> Clarion, Pennsylvania
> *ggoodman@clarion.edu*

To order other books in this series, please contact our Customer Service Department at:

> (800) 770-LANG (within the U.S.)
> (212) 647-7706 (outside the U.S.)
> (212) 647-7707 FAX

Or browse online by series at:

> www.peterlang.com